Editorial Project Manager
Erica N. Russikoff, M.A.

Editor in Chief
Karen J. Goldfluss, M.S. Ed.

Creative Director
Sarah M. Fournier

Cover Artist
Sarah Kim

Illustrator
Mark Mason

Art Coordinator
Renée Mc Elwee

Imaging
Amanda R. Harter

Publisher
Mary D. Smith, M.S. Ed.

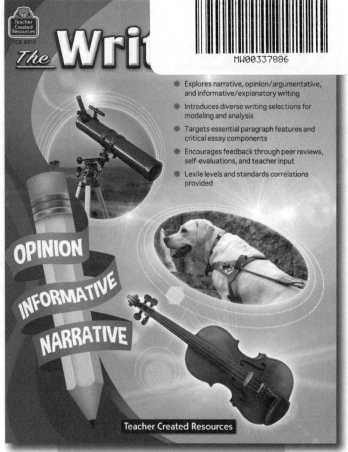

* Explores narrative, opinion/argumentative, and informative/explanatory writing
* Introduces diverse writing selections for modeling and analysis
* Targets essential paragraph features and critical essay components
* Encourages feedback through peer reviews, self-evaluations, and teacher input
* Lexile levels and standards correlations provided

Author
Tracie I. Heskett, M. Ed.

For correlations to the Common Core State Standards, see pages 157–160 of this book or visit *http://www.teachercreated.com/standards/*.

Teacher Created Resources
12621 Western Avenue
Garden Grove, CA 92841
www.teachercreated.com

ISBN: 978-1-4206-8015-7

© 2017 Teacher Created Resources
Made in U.S.A.

Cover photograph credits:
* Telescope, ©Ryan Wick (*https://www.flickr.com/photos/ryanwick/3461850112/*), CC BY 2.0.
* Guide dog, ©smerikal (*https://www.flickr.com/photos/smerikal/6059539899/*), CC BY-SA 2.0.
* Violin, public domain image.

Table of Contents

Introduction

The Write Stuff is a series designed to help students build strong foundational skills in writing. To master the skills needed to write effectively, students benefit from guided instruction, analysis of writing models, and writing for a variety of audiences. The books in this series guide both teachers and students through the process of writing as it relates to three specific writing formats.

This book provides writing samples for students to study, as well as opportunities for students to write their own pieces. Students receive feedback on their writing in a variety of ways. They participate in peer reviews, complete self-evaluations, receive evaluations from the teacher, and compare differences in these assessments of their writing.

About This Book

Sections: The book is divided into three main sections, one for each type of writing students need to learn for college and career readiness: Opinion/Argumentative Writing, Informative/ Explanatory Writing, and Narrative Writing.

THREE SECTIONS

Opinion/Argumentative Writing — Paragraph Module, Essay Module

Informative/Explanatory Writing — Paragraph Module, Essay Module

Narrative Writing — Paragraph Module, Essay Module

Themed Modules: Each section has two modules, or in-depth units.

First Module: This module presents a series of step-by-step lessons to introduce students to and teach the characteristics of that type of writing. Students read and discuss strong and weak examples of the type of writing in focus. Reading passages fall within the sixth-grade reading range based on Lexile estimates (925L–1070L) for this grade level. Students then model what they learned to write a piece in that specific genre, from opening sentence to conclusion.

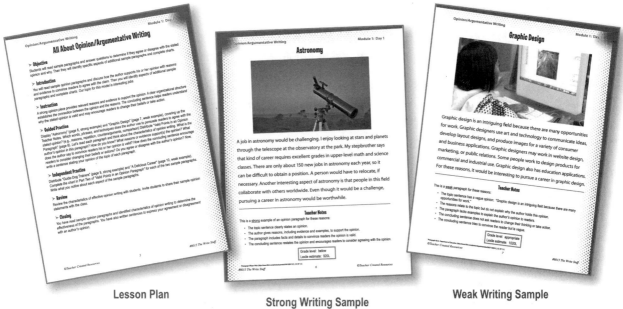

Lesson Plan   Strong Writing Sample   Weak Writing Sample

Second Module: This module provides additional experiences in which students learn about and practice writing a longer piece, or essay, in the focus genre. Each module suggests a topic for student writing. Additional related writing topics are listed at the back of the book on pages 155–156.

Note: Modules 1, 3, and 5 require 10 days or class periods to complete, while Modules 2, 4, and 6 require seven days.

A chart on pages 157–160 lists the Common Core State Standards addressed in each lesson.

How to Use This Book

Each module includes writing samples written below, at, and above grade level as indicated. Lessons suggest how to incorporate the writing samples, although you may use them in other ways for additional practice. For example, conduct a shared-writing activity in which students work together as a class to mimic a sample paragraph about the same or a different topic. Alternatively, have students work with a partner to strengthen an example of a weak paragraph. Students may also work independently to practice writing paragraphs using one or more strong examples as a model.

Each lesson begins with a scripted lesson plan. The script for the teacher is presented in italicized font. These lesson plans inform teachers about what to expect students to learn and be able to do. They enable teachers to make the best use of the time they have available for teaching writing in an already busy school day. The lessons include strategies that effectively help students learn to write.

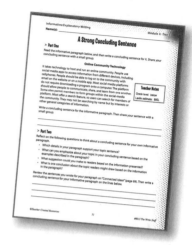

Within each module, student activities build on one another. Answers to activities are provided on the lesson plan. Students focus on a single topic throughout the module as they work toward a finished product. You may wish to have students keep their activity pages in a folder for reference as they complete each lesson. Alternatively, you may refer to the related topics on pages 155–156 to give students additional writing experiences during lesson activities.

Guided Practice provides opportunities for students to work together as a whole class, in small groups, or with partners to focus on a particular aspect of the writing type in focus. Independent Practice offers additional activities for students to apply new skills as they write one or more parts of the work in progress.

Each module has one lesson in which students participate in a peer-review activity. Encourage students to offer positive feedback as well as constructive criticism that will motivate their classmates to improve their writing.

Students complete a self-evaluation activity during each module and then later compare the scores they assigned their own writing with scores they receive on a teacher evaluation. Rubrics provide objective statements about writing that help students analyze and reflect on their work with the goal of creating written selections that are more effective and engaging for readers.

Some activities ask students to research their topics. Refer to the following topic overview chart to plan and provide appropriate research resources.

➤ Topics Overview

Opinion/Argumentative	Module 1	Interesting Jobs
Opinion/Argumentative	Module 2	Current Events or Issues
Informative/Explanatory	Module 3	Online Communities
Informative/Explanatory	Module 4	Virtual Reality
Narrative	Module 5	Volunteer Experiences
Narrative	Module 6	Nanotechnology

All About Opinion/Argumentative Writing

➤ Objective

Students will read sample paragraphs and answer questions to determine whether they agree or disagree with the stated opinion and why. Then they will identify specific aspects of additional sample paragraphs and complete charts.

➤ Introduction

You will read sample opinion paragraphs and discuss how the author supports his or her opinion with reasons and evidence to convince readers to agree with the claim. Then you will identify aspects of additional sample paragraphs and complete charts. Our topic for this module is interesting jobs.

➤ Instruction

A strong opinion piece provides relevant reasons and evidence to support the opinion. A clear organizational structure establishes the connection between the opinion and the reasons. The concluding sentence helps readers understand why the stated opinion is valid and may encourage readers to change their beliefs or take action.

➤ Guided Practice

Display "Astronomy" (page 6, strong example) and "Graphic Design" (page 7, weak example), covering up the Teacher Notes. *Which words, phrases, and techniques does the author use to persuade readers to agree with the stated opinion?* (e.g., reasons, repetition, counterarguments, comparison) Distribute "Valid Points in an Opinion Paragraph" (page 8). *Let's read each paragraph and think about the characteristics of opinion writing. What is the author's opinion in this paragraph? How do you know? What reasons or evidence support(s) the opinion? What does the author say to convince readers his or her opinion is valid? How does the concluding sentence encourage readers to consider changing their beliefs or actions? Do you agree or disagree with the author's opinion? Now, write a sentence stating your opinion of the topic of each paragraph.*

➤ Independent Practice

Distribute "Guide-Dog Trainers" (page 9, strong example) and "A Delicious Career" (page 10, weak example). *Complete the chart in Part Two of "Valid Points in an Opinion Paragraph" for each of the two sample paragraphs. Write what you notice about each aspect of the sample paragraphs.*

➤ Review

Review the characteristics of effective opinion writing with students. Invite students to share their sample opinion statements with the class.

➤ Closing

You have read sample opinion paragraphs and identified characteristics of opinion writing to determine the effectiveness of the paragraphs. You have also written sentences to express your agreement or disagreement with an author's opinion.

Astronomy

A job in astronomy would be challenging. I enjoy looking at stars and planets through the telescope at the observatory at the park. My stepbrother says that kind of career requires excellent grades in upper-level math and science classes. There are only about 150 new jobs in astronomy each year, so it can be difficult to obtain a position. A person would have to relocate, if necessary. Another interesting aspect of astronomy is that people in this field collaborate with others worldwide. Even though it would be a challenge, pursuing a career in astronomy would be worthwhile.

Teacher Notes

This is a <u>strong</u> example of an opinion paragraph for these reasons:

- The topic sentence clearly states an opinion.
- The author gives reasons, including evidence and examples, to support the opinion.
- The paragraph includes facts and details to convince readers the opinion is valid.
- The concluding sentence restates the opinion and encourages readers to consider agreeing with the opinion.

Grade level: below
Lexile estimate: 920L

Graphic Design

Graphic design is an intriguing field because there are many opportunities for work. Graphic designers use art and technology to communicate ideas, develop layout designs, and produce images for a variety of consumer and business applications. Graphic designers may work in website design, marketing, or public relations. Some people work to design products for commercial and industrial use. Graphic design also has education applications. For these reasons, it would be interesting to pursue a career in graphic design.

Teacher Notes

This is a <u>weak</u> paragraph for these reasons:

- The topic sentence has a vague opinion: "Graphic design is an intriguing field because there are many opportunities for work."
- The reasons relate to the topic but do not explain why the author holds this opinion.
- The paragraph lacks examples to explain the author's opinion to readers.
- The concluding sentence does not ask readers to change their thinking or take action.
- The concluding sentence tries to convince the reader but is vague.

Grade level: appropriate
Lexile estimate: 1020L

Name(s): _____

Valid Points in an Opinion Paragraph

➤ Part One

Think about your answers to the questions below as you read and discuss "Astronomy" (page 6) and "Graphic Design" (page 7) with classmates.

1. What is the author's opinion in this paragraph?
2. How do you know?
3. What reasons or evidence support(s) the opinion?
4. What does the author say to convince readers his or her opinion is valid?
5. How does the concluding sentence encourage readers to consider changing their beliefs or actions?
6. Do you agree or disagree with the author's opinion?

Write a sentence stating your opinion of the topic of "Astronomy."

_____

_____

Write a sentence stating your opinion of the topic of "Graphic Design."

_____

_____

➤ Part Two

Complete the chart for "Guide-Dog Trainers" (page 9) and "A Delicious Career" (page 10). Write what you notice about each aspect of the sample paragraphs.

Guide-Dog Trainers

Author's Opinion: _____

Reasons or Evidence: _____

Concluding Sentence: _____

_____

A Delicious Career

Author's Opinion: _____

Reasons or Evidence: _____

Concluding Sentence: _____

_____

Name(s): _____

Guide-Dog Trainers

There are few jobs more rewarding than being a guide-dog trainer. A guide-dog trainer works with puppies and can train them to help guide people who have vision difficulties. The trainer begins by teaching the puppy how to behave well in public. Next, the dog learns to follow complex commands in a variety of situations. Finally, the trainer teaches the visually impaired person the different commands the guide dog knows. Many trainers are sad when their dogs leave to go to their new owners. However, that is the best part of all because the trainer knows that for the rest of its life, the service animal will be a help to its new master.

Teacher Notes

Grade level: appropriate
Lexile estimate: 1010L

Name(s): _____

A Delicious Career

One of my passions is food; I enjoy preparing interesting, healthy food to eat. Often people will pursue a career in an area of particular interest to them. Career opportunities that involve food and nourishment include teaching people about healthy food, preparing meals, working in a bakery, and serving food to people. It would be great to earn money preparing healthy meals for families. I would also enjoy teaching people about nutrition and helping them plan their own interesting menus. It is fun to experiment with different cuisines from different regions and countries. Some people work their way up in the restaurant industry—from fast food to fine dining. Everyone has to eat, so the job possibilities are almost endless. If it involves food, the job would most certainly be interesting!

Teacher Notes

Grade level: below
Lexile estimate: 900L

Topic Sentences

➤ Objective

Students will write sample topic sentences about different topics and then comment on the effectiveness of classmates' sentences. They will also brainstorm topics for their opinion paragraphs and write sample topic sentences.

➤ Introduction

You will practice writing topic sentences about different topics and discuss with a partner what makes an effective topic sentence. Then you will brainstorm topics and write sample topic sentences for your own opinion paragraph.

➤ Instruction

A topic sentence introduces what the paragraph will be about in an interesting way. Readers can identify the specific focus of the topic of the paragraph. The author clearly states his or her opinion about the topic. The topic sentence is usually the first sentence. Interesting topic sentences catch readers' attention and raise questions in their minds, drawing them in, so they want to read more.

➤ Guided Practice

Distribute "My Opinions" (page 12). *Read each job description. On a separate piece of paper, write a topic sentence to introduce the subject (particular job) and your opinion about why it might be an interesting job. How can you write each sentence in a way to capture readers' attention? After you have written a topic sentence for each job, trade papers with a partner. Write comments on at least two of your partner's sentences to provide feedback on the effectiveness of his or her topic sentences.*

➤ Independent Practice

Distribute "An Interesting Topic Sentence" (page 13). *Complete Part One by thinking about the sample paragraphs you read earlier in this module as well as the sample topics you read about on "My Opinions." On a separate piece of paper, brainstorm ideas for an interesting job you would like to write about in your opinion paragraph. Draw a web or cluster to help you think of new and different ideas. Then choose one topic for your paragraph to complete the sentence frames.*

Complete Part Two by reading the list of techniques and checking one or two you would like to use when writing a topic sentence about a job that would be interesting for readers. Use your notes to write a topic sentence for your paragraph.

➤ Review

Review the characteristics of effective topic sentences and discuss students' sample topic sentences. Conduct a class discussion to help students brainstorm ideas for their opinion paragraphs as needed.

➤ Closing

You wrote sample topic sentences for different topics and gave and received comments. You also decided on a topic for your opinion paragraph and practiced writing topic sentences for your paragraph.

Name(s): _____

My Opinions

1. Read each job description.

2. On a separate piece of paper, write a topic sentence to introduce the subject (particular job) and your opinion about why it might be an interesting job. How can you write each sentence in a way to capture readers' attention?

3. After you have written a topic sentence for each job, trade papers with a partner.

4. Write comments on at least two of your partner's sentences to provide feedback on the effectiveness of his or her topic sentences.

Zookeeper

- works in a zoo, safari park, or aquarium
- prepares special diets for animals and feeds them
- gives baths and helps animals exercise
- cleans and maintains habitats
- observes animal behavior and health
- reports concerns to park managers
- answers questions from visitors

Astronaut

- coordinates shuttle operations including crew activities and supply maintenance
- works with shuttle systems
- understands mission requirements and objectives
- performs experiments
- takes part in activities outside the space shuttle

Musician

- performs at concerts
- plays in a recording studio to provide background music
- plays at events such as weddings
- plays in local restaurants
- may only work part-time
- may compose music for a specific group of people

Firefighter

- handles hazardous materials
- puts out wildfires
- puts out structural fires
- rescues people
- drives and maintains firefighting equipment

Name(s): _____

An Interesting Topic Sentence

➤ Part One

1. Think about the sample paragraphs you read earlier in this module as well as the sample topics you read about on "My Opinions" (page 12).

2. On a separate piece of paper, brainstorm ideas for an interesting job you would like to write about in your opinion paragraph. Draw a web or cluster to help you think of new and different ideas.

3. Choose one topic for your paragraph to complete the sentence frames below.

    _____ is an interesting job because

    _____

    _____.

    The particular aspect of this job I will focus on is _____

    _____

    _____.

➤ Part Two

Read the list of techniques below. Check one or two you would like to use to write a topic sentence about a job that would be interesting for readers.

- ☐ Introduce the particular point you want to make.
- ☐ Present an interesting fact related to your argument.
- ☐ State the topic clearly.
- ☐ Briefly tell why you hold this opinion.
- ☐ Give readers a preview of what will follow the statement.

Use your notes from above and your web or cluster to write a topic sentence for your paragraph.

_____

_____

_____

_____

Supporting Details

➤ Objective

Students will work in small groups to consider their audiences and the supporting details that would be relevant for those audiences. Then they will research their topics and take notes, including their sources. They will learn about different types of evidence and consider which types are most appropriate for their topics and audiences.

➤ Introduction

You will work with a small group to discuss your potential audience and the supporting details that will convince those readers your opinion is valid. You will learn about and research different types of evidence to include in your opinion paragraph.

➤ Instruction

People might be more likely to change their beliefs or behavior to agree with an author's opinion if it is well supported with reasons that include facts and details. Readers want to know why they should think or act a certain way. Effective argumentative writing supports the opinion in the topic sentence with facts and details that make sense. This evidence explains why the author's opinion is valid and helps convince readers to agree with the stated opinion. Reasons are presented in a logical order that leads naturally to the concluding sentence.

➤ Guided Practice

Distribute "Support Your Opinion" (page 15). *Share your topic sentence from "An Interesting Topic Sentence" (page 13) with a small group. Discuss potential audiences for your opinion paragraph. Who is your audience? What are the needs of the audience in relation to this topic? Which information and ideas should be included in your writing to meet the needs of your audience? What specific details will support your opinion and convince readers it is valid? Work with your small group to research specific information related to your topic. Document facts and details for your paragraph along with relevant sources.*

➤ Independent Practice

Distribute "Gather the Evidence" (page 16). *Authors use different types of evidence to support their claims and convince readers their stated opinions are valid. Read the description for each type of evidence. Then look back over your research notes on "Support Your Opinion." Which types of evidence have you gathered? Which type of evidence might be appropriate for your opinion paragraph? Continue your research to add details for the types of evidence you identified as helpful for your opinion paragraph. Write your notes and answers to the questions on a separate piece of paper.*

➤ Review

Review the types of evidence and provide examples of each, when possible. Discuss how these types of supporting details strengthen opinion writing.

➤ Closing

You researched supporting details for your opinion paragraph with a specific audience in mind. You also learned about different types of evidence to include in your opinion writing.

Name(s): _____

Support Your Opinion

Share your topic sentence from "An Interesting Topic Sentence" (page 13) with a small group. Then answer the following questions together. Take notes.

1. Who is your audience? What are the needs of the audience in relation to this topic?

    _____

    _____

2. Which information and ideas should be included in your writing to meet those needs and support your opinion?

    _____

    _____

    _____

3. What specific details will support your opinion and convince readers it is valid?

    _____

    _____

    _____

    _____

    _____

    _____

4. What should I research to support my reasons? What sources should I use? List them below.

    _____

    _____

    _____

    _____

    _____

    _____

    _____

    _____

Name(s): _____

Gather the Evidence

Read the description for each type of evidence.

Definitions	**Facts**
• Define key terms for readers • Help readers understand exactly what you are trying to say	• True information that can be proven • Something that actually happened • Something that is real

Personal Experiences	**Reasons**
• Based on your own or someone else's experiences • Not always reliable • Can add interest to the topic for readers	• An explanation • The motive behind someone's thought or action • Something that supports a thought and makes it valid • To show why it is right or valid

Expert Research or Opinions	**Statistics**
• Experts are people who have studied and researched a particular topic. • Sometimes experts in a field give their opinions. • These opinions may be based on their research.	• Data that shows the relationship between information and concepts • Expressed in numbers • Should be from a reliable source • Can be interpreted in different ways

Look back over your research notes on "Support Your Opinion" (page 15). Answer the following questions on another piece of paper.

- Which types of evidence have you gathered?

- Which types of evidence might be appropriate for your opinion paragraph?

- Continue your research to add details for the types of evidence you identified as helpful for your opinion paragraph.

Transition Words

➤ Objective

Students will identify and list transition words used in sample opinion paragraphs. They will use these words and others to write sentences with appropriate transitions for their own opinion paragraphs.

➤ Introduction

You will read sample opinion paragraphs and identify the transition words and phrases the author used. Then you will list the words and research to learn other transition words. You will also write sentences for your own paragraph with appropriate transition words.

➤ Instruction

Effective opinion writing includes reasons that support an opinion. Reasons explain why the author feels or thinks a certain way about a topic. Convincing reasons often include specific facts, details, or examples. Writers use transition words or phrases to connect reasons to the opinion in the topic sentence so that it all makes sense.

➤ Guided Practice

Distribute one or more sample paragraphs from Day 1 ("Astronomy" [page 6], "Graphic Design" [page 7], "Guide-Dog Trainers" [page 9], or "A Delicious Career" [page 10]) and "Observe Transitions" (page 18). *Complete Part One by working with a partner to identify the transition words in each paragraph. Look for the words in the word box and write any additional transition words you find in the paragraphs on the lines. Discuss with your partner how these words are used in sentences to connect opinions and reasons.*

➤ Independent Practice

Complete Part Two of "Observe Transitions." Use your notes from "Support Your Opinion" (page 15) and "Gather the Evidence" (page 16) to write sentences for your opinion paragraph. Think about how you will organize your paragraph. What types of transition words will make your writing flow smoothly and help readers follow your thinking? Include appropriate transition words in your sentences. Use the words from the word box, consulting additional reference materials as needed.

➤ Review

Review with students how transition words connect opinions and reasons in an opinion paragraph. Provide additional examples of transition words to assist students in writing sentences with transition words and phrases.

➤ Closing

You worked with a partner to identify and list transition words used in sample opinion paragraphs. Then you wrote sentences for your paragraph and included appropriate transition words and phrases.

Name(s): _____

Observe Transitions

➤ Part One

1. Review sample opinion paragraphs, such as "Astronomy" (page 6), "Graphic Design" (page 7), "Guide-Dog Trainers" (page 9), or "A Delicious Career" (page 10).

2. Work with a partner to identify the transition words in each paragraph.

3. Look for the words in the word box and write any additional transition words you find in the paragraphs on the lines.

4. Discuss with your partner how these words are used in sentences to connect opinions and reasons.

as	in addition	although	consequently
in the same way	specifically	for example	_____
similarly	in particular	for instance	_____
in contrast	otherwise	as a result	_____
moreover	instead	therefore	_____

➤ Part Two

- Use your notes from "Support Your Opinion" (page 15) and "Gather the Evidence" (page 16) to write sentences for your opinion paragraph on the lines below.

- Think about how you will organize your paragraph.

  What types of transition words will make your writing flow smoothly and help readers follow your thinking?

- Include appropriate transition words in your sentences. Use the words from the word box above, consulting additional reference materials as needed.

_____

_____

_____

_____

_____

_____

_____

_____

Concluding Sentences

➤ Objective

Students will observe concluding sentences in sample opinion paragraphs and form opinions about which sentences are most effective. They will discuss their opinions with classmates. Then they will write sample concluding sentences for their own opinion paragraphs.

➤ Introduction

You will read sample concluding sentences and form an opinion about which are effective and why. Then you will discuss your opinion with classmates. You will also practice writing concluding sentences for your own opinion paragraph.

➤ Instruction

A strong concluding sentence restates the opinion that was expressed in the topic sentence. One way to do this is to focus on the main idea. In the concluding sentence, the author states the logical decision or realization based on the reasons and evidence presented. A concluding sentence may state why the author holds the stated opinion or why he or she wrote the piece.

➤ Guided Practice

Distribute "An Effective Concluding Sentence" (page 20). *Read the concluding sentences in the sample opinion paragraphs from this module. Which sentences are effective? Why do you have that opinion? Draw a star by any concluding sentences you vote are effective.*

Then write the reason for your opinion on the lines below the paragraph. For Part Two, participate in a roundtable discussion with your small group. Use a timer or other device to ensure that each member of the group has an equal amount of time (for instance, two minutes) to express and discuss his or her opinion about the concluding sentences. Remember to explain why you hold a particular opinion about each concluding sentence.

➤ Independent Practice

Distribute "Write a Concluding Sentence" (page 21). *Complete Part One by looking back at the sample concluding sentences you have read in this module or from other resources. What do you notice about how the sentences are written? Summarize or list the reasons and evidence for your opinion from your own paragraph. Then, in Part Two, write concluding sentences for your opinion paragraph using two or more of the sentence frames. Use a separate piece of paper. In Part Three, read your topic sentence from "An Interesting Topic Sentence" (page 13). Now, reread the concluding sentences you wrote for Part Two. Choose one that best exemplifies a satisfactory concluding sentence. Rewrite both the topic and concluding sentences using different words.*

➤ Review

Review the characteristics of an effective opinion concluding sentence. If possible, display and discuss sample opinion paragraphs with concluding sentences that exhibit various characteristics, such as stating a logical decision, focusing on the main idea, or summarizing.

➤ Closing

You discussed with classmates your opinions about sample concluding sentences. Then you practiced writing concluding sentences for your opinion paragraph about an interesting job.

An Effective Concluding Sentence

➤ Part One

1. Read samples of concluding sentences in opinion paragraphs from this module.
2. Which sentences are effective? Why do you have that opinion? Draw a star by any concluding sentences you vote are effective.
3. Write the reason for your opinion on the lines below each paragraph.

A job in astronomy would be challenging. I enjoy looking at stars and planets through the telescope at the observatory at the park. My stepbrother says that kind of career requires excellent grades in upper-level math and science classes. There are only about 150 new jobs in astronomy each year, so it can be difficult to obtain a position. A person would have to relocate, if necessary. Another interesting aspect of astronomy is that people in this field collaborate with others worldwide. Even though it would be a challenge, pursuing a career in astronomy would be worthwhile.

_____

_____

Graphic design is an intriguing field because there are many opportunities for work. Graphic designers use art and technology to communicate ideas, develop layout designs, and produce images for a variety of consumer and business applications. Graphic designers may work in website design, marketing, or public relations. Some people work to design products for commercial and industrial use. Graphic design also has education applications. For these reasons, it would be interesting to pursue a career in graphic design.

_____

_____

One of my passions is food; I enjoy preparing interesting, healthy food to eat. Often people will pursue a career in an area of particular interest to them. Career opportunities that involve food and nourishment include teaching people about healthy food, preparing meals, working in a bakery, and serving food to people. It would be great to earn money preparing healthy meals for families. I would also enjoy teaching people about nutrition and helping them plan their own interesting menus. It is fun to experiment with different cuisines from different regions and countries. Some people work their way up in the restaurant industry—from fast food to fine dining. Everyone has to eat, so the job possibilities are almost endless. If it involves food, the job would most certainly be interesting!

_____

_____

➤ Part Two

Participate in a roundtable discussion with your small group. Use a timer or other device to ensure that each member of the group has an equal amount of time to express and discuss his or her opinion about the concluding sentences above.

Write a Concluding Sentence

➤ Part One

Look back at the sample concluding sentences you have read in this module or from other resources. What do you notice about how the sentences are written?

_____

_____

Summarize or list the reasons and evidence for your opinion from your own paragraph.

① _____

_____

② _____

_____

③ _____

_____

➤ Part Two

On a separate piece of paper, write concluding sentences for your opinion paragraph. Use two or more of the sentence frames below to practice.

- For these reasons, _____.
- In conclusion, I think _____ is interesting because _____.
- Even though _____, I think _____.
- In summary, _____ is an interesting job because _____.
- You might want to _____ since _____.

➤ Part Three

Read your topic sentence from "An Interesting Topic Sentence" (page 13). Now, reread the concluding sentences you wrote for Part Two. Choose one that best exemplifies a satisfactory concluding sentence. Below, rewrite both the topic and concluding sentences using different words.

Topic Sentence

_____

_____

Concluding Sentence

_____

_____

First Draft and Peer Review

➤ Objective

Students will write first drafts of their opinion paragraphs and work with partners to review their writing using a checklist of characteristics. Then they will read their paragraphs aloud and ask and answer questions to strengthen their writing.

➤ Introduction

Today you will use your notes and writing on activity pages from this module to write a first draft of your opinion paragraph. Then you will use a checklist to review your paragraph with a partner and ask and answer questions to clarify and strengthen your writing.

➤ Instruction

A draft is not the finished piece. It is a rough copy, a place where you refer to any notes and write your ideas as sentences and paragraphs. Remember to begin with a topic sentence that includes an opinion; include reasons, facts, and details; and finish with a concluding sentence. Use transition words and phrases to connect your reasons to your opinion. During the drafting process, we revise our writing to make it stronger. In opinion writing, we want to convince our readers to agree with our opinion or take a particular action.

Often people review writing others have done. A review might analyze the writing based on specific characteristics. The reviewer may also consider the content, or the merits, of what the author has to say. When we review others' writing, we think about the strengths and weaknesses of the piece and why we might recommend others read it.

➤ Guided Practice

Use your notes and activity pages from this module to write a first draft of your opinion paragraph.

Distribute "Check My Writing" (page 23). *The checklist in Part One lists characteristics of effective opinion writing. Read your partner's paragraph silently to yourself. Then check off or comment on each characteristic as it applies to your partner's writing.*

➤ Independent Practice

As you read your partner's writing, offer positive and constructive feedback. Everyone likes to hear what they've done right. Remember to be kind and specific, stay on task, and thank your partner. Take turns reading your paragraph aloud to your partner. Ask your partner to write response questions after you read aloud. Use the questions to identify places where your writing needs additional detail to clarify for readers.

➤ Review

Discuss the impact revising can have on the writing process. Review and discuss the characteristics of effective opinion writing as listed on the chart on "Check My Writing" before students review their classmates' work.

➤ Closing

You wrote a first draft of your opinion paragraph about interesting jobs. Then you reviewed a classmate's writing and asked your partner to write response questions to think about ways to make your opinion writing more effective.

Check My Writing

➤ Part One

The checklist below lists characteristics of effective opinion writing.

1. Read your partner's paragraph silently to yourself.

2. Check off or comment on each characteristic as it applies to your partner's writing.

Checklist	Comment
The topic sentence clearly states the author's opinion about the topic.	
The topic sentence introduces what the paragraph will be about in an interesting way.	
The reasons support the author's opinion.	
The reasons help convince readers to agree with the stated opinion.	
The reasons include facts, details, and examples.	
The reasons are presented in a logical order that leads naturally to the concluding sentence.	
The transition words or phrases connect the reasons, facts, and details to the opinion in the topic sentence.	
The concluding sentence restates the author's opinion or main idea.	
The concluding sentence may state a logical decision or realization based on the reasons presented.	
The concluding sentence may state why the author holds the stated opinion or why he or she wrote the piece.	

➤ Part Two

1. Take turns reading your paragraph aloud to your partner.

2. Ask your partner to write response questions on a separate piece of paper.

3. Use the questions to identify places where your writing needs additional detail to clarify for readers.

Second Draft and Self-Evaluation

➤ Objective

Students will work in small groups to complete a series of steps to evaluate the first drafts of their opinion paragraphs and write second drafts. Then they will use a rubric to evaluate their second drafts.

➤ Introduction

You will work with a small group to follow a series of steps to evaluate your first draft. Then you will use your notes to write a second draft of your opinion paragraph. You will use a rubric to evaluate and score your second draft on the characteristics of opinion writing.

➤ Instruction

The drafting part of the writing process happens when we focus on ways to make our writing better. A checklist of characteristics is a helpful tool to use to identify strengths and weaknesses in an opinion piece. One particular type of checklist is called a rubric. The rubric you will use today lists each characteristic of opinion writing as a separate category. Different levels of quality are described for each characteristic with a score for each level.

➤ Guided Practice

Distribute "Steps to Great Writing" (page 25). *Work with a small group to complete the evaluation process steps described. Then use any notes you have written on your first draft, along with the feedback you received on the peer review, to write a second draft. Use the checklist of characteristics on "Check My Writing" (page 23) to focus on specific aspects of opinion writing.*

➤ Independent Practice

When we evaluate something, we look at it carefully to see what is good and valuable in it. Today we will think about how we incorporated aspects of effective opinion writing. It's also important to note areas in which we are still learning and need more practice. Distribute "Self-Evaluation: Opinion Paragraph" (page 26). *This rubric shows the characteristics I will look for when I read your opinion paragraphs. Use this page as a guide to help you evaluate and score your second draft. Write notes about areas you would like to strengthen when you write a final draft.*

➤ Review

Discuss the impact revising can have on the writing process. Review the categories on the rubric, discussing the qualities of writing that correspond to the scores for each category.

➤ Closing

You followed a series of steps to evaluate and revise the first draft of your opinion paragraph and wrote a second draft. Then you used a rubric to evaluate your second draft for the characteristics of effective opinion writing.

Name(s): _____

Steps to Great Writing

Work with a small group of classmates to complete the following evaluation process.

1. Read your paragraph.

2. Ask questions about your writing, such as, "How effective is my writing?" and "Will readers be convinced to agree with my opinion?"

3. Review the feedback you received and your notes on the "Check My Writing" (page 23) peer review.

4. Solve any problems you observed. How can you test the effectiveness of your writing? Based on the evidence you presented, does your argument stand as valid?

5. Use the answers to your questions, along with your notes from the peer review, to evaluate your writing.

6. Use the changes suggested by the answers to your questions and your notes from the peer review to write a second draft of your opinion paragraph below.

_____

_____

_____

_____

_____

_____

_____

_____

_____

_____

_____

_____

_____

_____

_____

_____

_____

Self-Evaluation: Opinion Paragraph

Name: _____   Score: _____

	4	3	2	1
Topic Sentence	My topic sentence clearly states my opinion about an interesting job and introduces my specific topic in an interesting way.	My topic sentence states my opinion and is related to my topic.	My topic sentence states an opinion I have about a job.	My topic sentence does not state an opinion and/or is not related to the topic.
Organization	I organized my paragraph with related ideas grouped together to explain why I hold this opinion about my topic.	I grouped some related ideas to support my opinion about an interesting job.	My ideas support my opinion, but they are not organized in any particular order.	My ideas do not support or explain my opinion in a way that would convince readers.
Reasons and Evidence	My paragraph includes reasons that clearly support my opinion about an interesting job with relevant evidence, including facts and details.	My paragraph includes reasons that support my opinion about an interesting job with some facts and details.	My paragraph includes reasons and a few details about a job.	My reasons are not related to my opinion or the topic of a job and do not include details.
Transition Words	My opinion and supporting reasons are connected in a logical way with appropriate transition words and phrases.	My opinion and supporting reasons are connected with transition words and phrases.	Some of my reasons are connected to my opinion with transition words and phrases.	My reasons are not connected in any way to my opinion.
Concluding Sentence	My paragraph has a concluding sentence that is directly related to my opinion about an interesting job and challenges readers to change the way they think or behave.	My paragraph has a concluding sentence that is related to my opinion about an interesting job and considers the reader.	My paragraph has a concluding sentence that is related to my opinion or says something about a job.	My concluding sentence is not related to my opinion and is not about a job.

26

Final Draft

➤ Objective

Students will learn and practice using proofreading symbols to edit their second drafts. They will then write final drafts of their opinion paragraphs.

➤ Introduction

You will learn how to use proofreading symbols to edit your writing to make it as correct as possible. Then you will write a final draft of your opinion paragraph.

➤ Instruction

A final draft is the finished piece that we will share with others. You may have heard this referred to as "publishing." Publishing includes the idea that the work will be made available to others in some format. A published piece should be the best possible work of an author, which includes correct conventions.

➤ Guided Practice

Authors use proofreading marks to make notes about revisions they want to make to their writing. Display "Proofreading Symbols" (page 28) and discuss with students. Cover and reveal the right-hand column as you discuss each mark with the class. Discuss each symbol and/or purpose or definition. *When and why do we use each symbol on this chart to edit our writing? Which marks will be easiest for you to remember and use? Why? Which marks will be more difficult for you to incorporate into your editing? Why?*

How will you publish your final draft and who will be your audience?

➤ Independent Practice

Distribute "Proofreading Symbols." *Work with a partner to use the proofreading marks to edit the second draft of your essay. Ask your partner if you need help understanding how to use any of the marks. Which areas of editing or proofreading are your strengths? How can you help your partner identify these changes they might need to make in their writing? Make the necessary corrections to your second draft and use a word-processing program or other digital means to produce a final draft of your opinion paragraph.*

➤ Review

Discuss the importance of editing and revising writing; clear, correct writing is easier for readers to understand. Clarify proofreading marks, demonstrating how to use them in sample text, as necessary.

➤ Closing

You worked with a partner to use proofreading symbols to edit your second draft and then wrote a final draft with correct conventions to publish your writing for an audience.

Name(s): _____

Proofreading Symbols

Editor's Mark	Meaning	Example
≡	capitalize	they fished in lake tahoe.
/	make it lowercase	Five Students missed the Bus.
sp.	spelling mistake	The day was clowdy and cold.
⊙	add a period	Tomorrow is a holiday⊙
ℓ	delete (remove)	One person knew the the answer.
∧	add a word	Six were in the litter.
⟨,⟩	add a comma	He planted peas corn, and squash.
∼	reverse words or letters	An otter swam in the bed kelp.
⟨'⟩	add an apostrophe	The child's bike was blue.
⟨"⟩ ⟨"⟩	add quotation marks	Why can't I go? she cried.
#	make a space	He ate two redapples.
⌣	close the space	Her favorite game is soft ball.
⌗	begin a new paragraph	to know. Next on the list

Final Evaluation

➤ Objective

Students will record their self-evaluation scores and the scores they received on the teacher evaluation. They will give and receive feedback from partners as they review the evaluations and compare the scores.

➤ Introduction

You will record the scores from your self-evaluation and the evaluation you received from me to compare the scores. You will give and receive a different perspective and reflect on the insight such evaluations provide about your writing.

➤ Instruction

A rubric lists the qualities that make writing effective. Increasing levels of quality receive higher scores on a point scale. Reading the descriptions of these levels helps us know how we can improve our writing. Display "Teacher Evaluation: Opinion Paragraph" (page 30). *How does the rubric correspond to the characteristics of effective opinion writing we've practiced?* Discuss with students.

➤ Guided Practice

Distribute marked copies of "Teacher Evaluation: Opinion Paragraph," students' completed self-evaluations ("Self-Evaluation: Opinion Paragraph" [page 26]), and "Different Perspectives" (page 31). *In Part One of "Different Perspectives," record the scores you gave your writing on "Self-Evaluation: Opinion Paragraph." Record the scores you received on "Teacher Evaluation: Opinion Paragraph." In Part Two, trade papers with a partner. Review the scores your partner received from the teacher and write a paragraph about your evaluation of your partner's writing based on the scores.*

➤ Independent Practice

Complete Part Three by reviewing the scores you received on "Teacher Evaluation: Opinion Paragraph." Summarize the evaluation you received from the teacher in a few sentences on a separate piece of paper. Then answer the questions to compare your partner's perspective of the evaluation you received from the teacher with your perspective. How does your partner's perspective help you better understand the scores you received from the teacher? What did you learn about your writing from these different perspectives (your partner's, the evaluation scores you received from me, and your own perspective of the evaluation you received)? How will this new insight help you strengthen your writing?

➤ Review

Review the categories on each scoring rubric and point out how they are the same, only with slightly different wording to reflect the point of view of the person scoring the writing (student and teacher). Answer any questions about the rubric and writing scores students received.

➤ Closing

You reviewed the scores you gave your opinion paragraph on a self-evaluation and the scores you received from the teacher. You read a classmate's interpretation of the scores and compared that with your own perspective to gain new insights on how to strengthen your writing.

Teacher Evaluation: Opinion Paragraph

Student Name: _____   **Score:** _____

	4	3	2	1
Topic Sentence	The topic sentence clearly states the author's opinion about an interesting job and introduces a specific topic in an interesting way.	The topic sentence states the author's opinion and is related to the topic.	The topic sentence states an opinion the author has about a job.	The topic sentence does not state an opinion and/or is not related to the topic.
Organization	The author organized the paragraph with related ideas grouped together to explain why he or she holds this opinion about the topic.	The author grouped some related ideas to support his or her opinion about an interesting job.	The author's ideas support his or her opinion, but they are not organized in any particular order.	The author's ideas do not support or explain his or her opinion in a way that would convince readers.
Reasons and Evidence	The paragraph includes reasons that clearly support the author's opinion about an interesting job with relevant evidence, including facts and details.	The paragraph includes reasons that support the author's opinion about an interesting job with some facts and details.	The paragraph includes reasons and a few details about a job.	The reasons are not related to the author's opinion or the topic of a job and do not include details.
Transition Words	The author's opinion and supporting reasons are connected in a logical way with appropriate transition words and phrases.	The author's opinion and supporting reasons are connected with transition words and phrases.	Some of the author's reasons are connected to the opinion with transition words and phrases.	The author's reasons are not connected in any way to the opinion.
Concluding Sentence	The paragraph has a concluding sentence that is directly related to the author's opinion about an interesting job and challenges readers to change the way they think or behave.	The paragraph has a concluding sentence that is related to the author's opinion about an interesting job and considers the reader.	The paragraph has a concluding sentence that is related to the author's opinion or says something about a job.	The concluding sentence is not related to the author's opinion and is not about a job.

Name(s): _____

Different Perspectives

➤ Part One

- Record the scores you gave your writing on "Self-Evaluation: Opinion Paragraph" (page 26).
- Record the scores you received on "Teacher Evaluation: Opinion Paragraph" (page 30).

Self-Evaluation Scores	Rubric Category	Teacher Evaluation Scores
	Topic Sentence	
	Organization	
	Reasons and Evidence	
	Transition Words	
	Concluding Sentence	

➤ Part Two

- Trade papers with a partner.
- Review the scores your partner received from the teacher and write a paragraph on a separate piece of paper about your evaluation of your partner's writing based on the scores.

➤ Part Three

- Return your partner's paper.
- Review the scores you received on "Teacher Evaluation: Opinion Paragraph."
- Summarize the evaluation you received from the teacher in a few sentences on a separate piece of paper.
- Answer the following questions to compare your partner's perspective of the evaluation you received from the teacher with your perspective:

1. How does your partner's perspective help you better understand the scores you received from the teacher?

   _____

   _____

2. What did you learn about your writing from these different perspectives (your partner's, the evaluation scores you received from the teacher, and your own perspective of the evaluation you received)?

   _____

   _____

3. How will this new insight help you strengthen your writing?

   _____

   _____

Review

➤ Objective

Students will read and discuss the characteristics of strong opinion writing in a sample paragraph. Then they will read a second paragraph and identify specific characteristics of opinion writing.

➤ Introduction

You will read sample paragraphs and identify and discuss the characteristics of opinion writing in each.

➤ Instruction

When we review something, we look at it again. This helps us to remember what we've learned. Opinion writing, by definition, has a clear statement of opinion. It is writing in which an author states a particular point of view about a topic. The author supports the opinion in the topic sentence with related reasons and evidence, such as facts and details. A concluding sentence restates the topic sentence and/or convinces the reader to agree or take action.

➤ Guided Practice

Display "Technical Trainers" (page 33), covering up the Teacher Notes. *What characteristics of strong opinion writing do you notice in this paragraph? What is the topic? What is the author's opinion of the topic? How do you know? Which evidence and details are facts? Which are opinions? How do each contribute to the argument that the author's opinion is valid? Do you agree or disagree with the opinion? Why or why not? What would you change or strengthen in this paragraph?*

➤ Independent Practice

Distribute "Review the Characteristics of Opinion Writing" (page 34). *Read the sample paragraph. What characteristics of opinion writing does this paragraph demonstrate? Underline and/or circle the words and phrases that demonstrate each characteristic of opinion writing. Draw a line to match the text you marked with the appropriate characteristic listed in the column on the right. Discuss your answers and reasoning with a partner.*

➤ Review

Review the characteristics of opinion writing and go over students' responses to the matching activity as necessary.

➤ Closing

You read samples of opinion writing and discussed how each paragraph demonstrated specific characteristics of opinion writing.

Technical Trainers

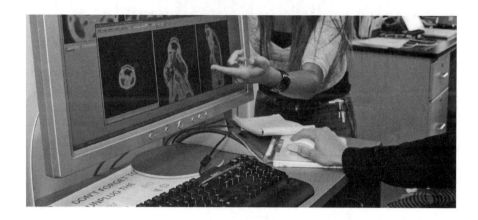

People who work as technical trainers have a different perspective on technology. Not only do they use technology, but they teach others how to use computers and other devices. Even those with very well-paying jobs may not know much about the technology their job requires them to use. Technical trainers teach CEOs, teachers, chairmen, and many other important people. They may even train their bosses! This is because not everyone knows how to use different kinds of technical devices, such as computers, tablets, or phones. Unsure of their abilities, some people lack confidence and may be hesitant to use technology. Technical trainers help people use technology to perform the required tasks and duties of their jobs. If you ever get a job as a technical trainer, just remember to smile. You and your pupil can each learn from each other!

Teacher Notes

This paragraph has the following characteristics of opinion writing:

- The topic sentence includes the topic of the paragraph and the author's opinion of the topic.
- The evidence includes details and examples to support the author's opinion.
- The paragraph is organized in a way that makes sense.
- The concluding sentence appeals to the reader.

Grade level: appropriate
Lexile estimate: 960L

Name(s): _____

Review the Characteristics of Opinion Writing

1. Underline and/or circle the words and phrases that demonstrate each characteristic of opinion writing.

2. Draw a line to match the text you marked with the appropriate characteristic listed in the column on the right.

3. Discuss your answers and reasoning with a partner.

The position of receptionist fulfills a vital role in an organization. A receptionist often provides visitors with their first impressions of the company. They welcome visitors in person or on the phone, answer emails, and direct visitors to appropriate people and departments. Receptionists also make appointments, maintain common areas, and coordinate calendars. In this digital age, receptionists have the option of keeping all this information in the cloud, but usually, they keep it all in their brains. The job can be very hard, but it is wonderful for multitaskers. If you want to multitask and interact with many different people, this is the job for you.	The topic sentence clearly states an opinion. The author gives reasons, including evidence and examples, to support the opinion. The paragraph includes facts and details to convince readers the opinion is valid. The organizational structure makes connections between the author's opinion and the reasons. The concluding sentence restates the opinion and encourages readers to consider agreeing with the opinion.

Teacher Notes

Grade level: appropriate
Lexile estimate: 990L

Introductory Paragraphs

➤ Objective

Students will identify effective thesis statements and practice writing thesis statements. They will then use a diagram to consider the main points of their essays. Students will also write sample sentences to engage readers and draft introductory paragraphs.

➤ Introduction

You will identify effective thesis statements and write your own thesis statement. You will then use a diagram to consider your approach to the main points in your argument. You will also write sample sentences to engage readers and draft an introductory paragraph for your opinion essay. Our topic for this module is current events or issues.

➤ Instruction

An opinion paragraph has a stated opinion, usually in the first sentence. In an opinion essay, the topic sentence is also called the thesis statement. The thesis statement is provided in an introductory paragraph, but it may or may not be the first sentence. A thesis statement introduces the author's opinion about the topic and the reasons that support that claim. The first sentence should capture readers' attention.

➤ Guided Practice

What is our prompt for this module? (Write an opinion essay about a current event or issue.) *What is it asking you to do?* (express an opinion in essay format) *Which main points about your chosen topic will your essay address? Which reasons and evidence will you use to support your opinion?* Discuss possible current events and issues for student essay topics.

The introductory paragraph of an essay contains a thesis statement. Photocopy "Effective Thesis Statements" (page 36), covering up the answers. Distribute the activity page. *Read the sample thesis statements in Part One. Which thesis statements are effective? Why or why not? Which issue from the class discussion most interests you? How could you learn more about that issue? Write your topic and then write a sentence to express your opinion about that topic. Use the thesis statements you identified as effective in Part One as a guide when completing Part Two.*

➤ Independent Practice

Distribute "Perspectives on My Topic" (page 37). *Use the diagram to plan an overview of your essay. Review the main points you want to make in your argument. These should be listed briefly in your thesis statement on "Effective Thesis Statements." Write your topic and opinion in the center hexagon. You might choose to simply rewrite your thesis statement. Using the back of the page or a separate piece of paper, write several sentences about each of the six points of view on your subject described in the diagram.*

Distribute "A Captivating Introductory Paragraph" (page 38). *How will you capture readers' attention? In Part One of this activity, you will practice writing sentences that demonstrate different ways authors engage their readers. Write a sample sentence related to your topic to capture readers' attention for each type of sentence. Trade papers with a partner. Write a comment about your partner's sample sentences and discuss your responses. Refer to your notes from Part One to complete Part Two, in which you will draft an introductory paragraph for your opinion essay. Then use the checklist as a guide to review your introductory paragraph.*

➤ Review

Review and discuss students' responses on "Effective Thesis Statements." Explain and discuss possible perspectives on "Perspectives on My Topic" for a sample topic, as needed.

➤ Closing

You reviewed sample thesis statements and then wrote a thesis statement for your chosen topic. You considered the main points of your essay, wrote sample sentences to capture readers' attention, and drafted your introductory paragraph.

Name(s): _____

Effective Thesis Statements

➤ Part One

Read each thesis statement and draw a star next to those that are examples of a strong thesis statement. On the line below each statement, write why it is or is not an effective thesis statement.

1. A committee comprised of students, parents, school administrators, and nutritionists should make decisions about food served at school.

    _____

    _____

2. Commemorating anniversaries of historic events helps people understand their significance, honors those involved, and strengthens our culture.

    _____

    _____

3. Weather forecasts and news coverage are ways people can prepare for and stay safe during severe weather events.

    _____

    _____

4. People need healthcare, but not everyone agrees on the best way to provide it.

    _____

    _____

5. Everyone should vote because this enables people to exercise one of their rights as citizens, become familiar with the issues facing our society, and express opinions.

    _____

    _____

➤ Part Two

What is your topic? _____

What is your opinion about your topic? _____

Write a thesis statement for your opinion essay. Use the thesis statements you identified as effective in Part One as a guide.

_____

_____

Answers
Part One: 1. Yes, because it expresses an opinion and presents an overview of main ideas for the body of the essay; 2. Yes, because it presents a specific, debatable claim and provides an overview of the points the essay will address; 3. No, because it expresses an opinion but is not easily debatable and lacks specifics or an overview; 4. No, because it expresses an opinion, but it is vague, and the sentence lacks specifics or an overview of main points; 5. Yes, because it expresses an opinion and provides specific points for argument within the body of the essay.

Name(s): _____

Perspectives on My Topic

Use the diagram below to plan an overview of your essay.

- Review the main points you want to make in your argument.
- Write your topic and opinion in the center hexagon.
- On the back of this page or a separate piece of paper, write several sentences about each of the six points of view on your subject described in the diagram.

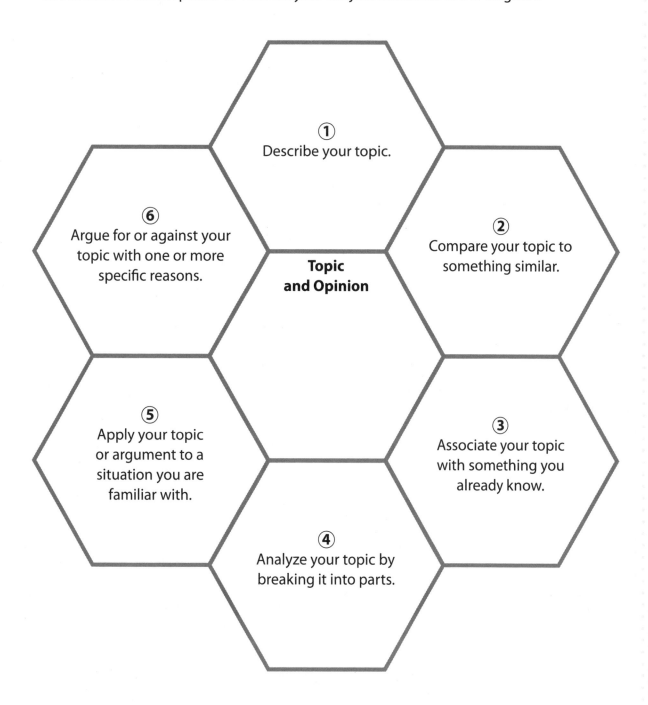

① Describe your topic.

② Compare your topic to something similar.

③ Associate your topic with something you already know.

④ Analyze your topic by breaking it into parts.

⑤ Apply your topic or argument to a situation you are familiar with.

⑥ Argue for or against your topic with one or more specific reasons.

Topic and Opinion

Name(s): _____

A Captivating Introductory Paragraph

➤ Part One

Write a sample sentence related to your topic to capture readers' attention for each type of sentence.

1. Write a sentence addressed to your reader.

_____

_____

2. Begin with a related quotation.

_____

_____

3. Ask a question to get readers thinking about the topic.

_____

_____

Trade papers with a partner. Write a comment about how well each of your partner's sample sentences captures your attention and why. Then discuss your responses with your partner.

_____

_____

➤ Part Two

1. Refer to your notes from Part One to draft an introductory paragraph for your opinion essay. Continue on a separate piece of paper, if necessary.

_____

_____

_____

_____

2. Use the checklist below as a guide to review your introductory paragraph.

Does my paragraph . . .

☐ include a sentence that captures readers' attention, so they will want to continue reading the essay?

☐ have a thesis statement that states my opinion about the topic and gives an overview of two or more main points that will be discussed in the essay?

☐ introduce the topic and provide sufficient background information for readers?

☐ introduce why the topic is important or significant for readers?

Body Paragraphs

➤ Objective

Students will research evidence about the main points of their essays. They will also survey classmates to learn others' opinions of their topics.

➤ Introduction

You will review your thesis statement and then research your topic. You will also learn about opposing arguments and survey classmates to learn their opinions of your topic.

➤ Instruction

It is important to learn to express our opinions in acceptable ways and to explain our logic. Our arguments may not always convince people to agree with our opinion, but they show we have reasonably thought through why we think a particular way. Each paragraph in the body of your essay explains and supports one of the reasons introduced in the introductory paragraph. Develop each main point with evidence that supports your opinion. Evidence includes facts, details, and examples that show readers why your opinion is valid. Sometimes authors will include an opposing argument. Transition words and phrases will help readers understand the connections between each reason and the author's stated opinion.

➤ Guided Practice

Distribute "Supporting Evidence" (page 40). *Reread your thesis statement from "Effective Thesis Statements" (page 36) and your notes on "Perspectives on My Topic" (page 37). Review the main points you plan to address in your essay. Use your notes to think about your topic and argument in a familiar context. Which types of evidence will you use to convince readers your opinion and arguments are valid? Research your topic and note details from various sources of evidence that pertain to your argument. If you don't have room to list all the bibliographic information for each source, use a numbering system to code your sources and list the bibliographic information on a separate piece of paper.*

➤ Independent Practice

Distribute "Develop an Opposing Argument" (page 41). *Read the information in Part One about how to address an opposing argument in an opinion essay. Discuss what you learned with a partner. In Part Two, write a question to ask classmates to survey their opinions of your topic. Interview several classmates to investigate the beliefs of others about your topic. Write each person's response in the appropriate column of the chart. Then read through the responses to develop a logical opposing argument related to your opinion of the topic or issue addressed in your essay.*

➤ Review

Review "Gather the Evidence" (from Module 1, page 16) for further explanation of each source of evidence. Demonstrate how to list bibliographic information for sources.

➤ Closing

You researched information and evidence about your topic. You discussed the role of opposing arguments with a partner, then surveyed classmates to learn their opinions of your topic to develop an opposing argument paragraph to include in your opinion essay.

Name(s): _____

Supporting Evidence

1. Reread your thesis statement from "Effective Thesis Statements" (page 36) and your notes on "Perspectives on My Topic" (page 37).

2. Review the main points you plan to address in your essay. Use your notes to think about your topic and argument in a familiar context.

3. Research your topic and note details from various sources of evidence that pertain to your argument.

4. If you don't have room to list all the bibliographic information for each source, use a numbering system to code your sources and list the bibliographic information on a separate piece of paper.

Evidence	Details	Sources
Personal Experiences		
Definitions		
Facts		
Reasons		
Statistics		
Expert Research or Opinions		

Develop an Opposing Argument

➤ Part One

Often an opinion essay acknowledges the opposing viewpoint. This allows readers to consider the issue from multiple perspectives. The author and readers can then better understand the strengths and weaknesses of the stated opinion. This results in a more logical argument of a specific claim.

Read the information below about how to address an opposing argument in an opinion essay. Discuss what you learned with a partner.

- Acknowledge the opposing argument.
- Explain how and why it does not align with your thesis statement.
- Present the opposing argument objectively and accurately.
- Acknowledge strengths of the opposition and point out weaknesses.
- Allow readers to draw their own conclusions.

Reasons an opposing argument may not be valid:

- outdated
- based on incorrect information
- lacks strength or significance
- misinterpretation of facts

➤ Part Two

1. Write a question to ask classmates to survey their opinions of your topic.

   _____

   _____

2. Interview classmates to investigate the beliefs of others about your topic.

3. Write each classmate's response in the appropriate column of the chart.

4. On a separate piece of paper, draft an opposing-argument paragraph related to your opinion of the topic or issue addressed in your essay.

Argument	Opposing Argument

Concluding Paragraphs

➤ Objective

Students will read a sample opinion essay, discuss it in small groups, and write concluding paragraphs for the essay. They will also write concluding paragraphs for their own opinion essays and give and receive feedback with partners about their concluding paragraphs.

➤ Introduction

You will read and discuss a sample opinion essay in a small group. Then you will write a sample concluding paragraph for the essay. You will also write a concluding paragraph for your own opinion essay and offer and receive feedback with a partner.

➤ Instruction

The concluding paragraph summarizes the opinion in the thesis statement and the reasons for the author's opinion. In this paragraph, the author concludes the argument and tries to convince readers that the stated opinion is valid. Concluding paragraphs may follow one of several different formats:

- *a summary, which provides readers with an overview of the topic and the reasons for the author's opinion*
- *a prompt for readers to think more about the issue*
- *a rhetorical question or a quotation related to the topic*
- *a comparison of the author's conclusion to another situation*
- *a description of results, consequences, or warnings related to readers' behavior*
- *a specific call to action*

➤ Guided Practice

Distribute "Significant Historic Events" (page 43). *Work with a small group to discuss the questions. Then, on a separate piece of paper, write a concluding paragraph for this opinion essay. Which features of a concluding paragraph could you add to engage readers and convince them to agree with the author's opinion? Which main approach did each group member take in writing their sample concluding paragraph?* (summarize, convince, offer readers something to think about, call to action or change in belief) *Share your thoughts and writing with your group.*

➤ Independent Practice

Distribute "An Engaging Concluding Paragraph" (page 44). *Review the introductory paragraph and body paragraphs you wrote for your opinion essay in previous activities.*

Write a concluding paragraph for your essay. Trade papers with a partner and whisper-read your partner's concluding paragraph. Then answer the questions to provide feedback to your partner.

➤ Review

Discuss sample concluding paragraphs from classroom resources to identify examples of techniques authors use to engage and convince readers.

➤ Closing

You read a sample opinion essay and wrote a related concluding paragraph based on the author's topic and opinion. Then you wrote a concluding paragraph for your opinion essay and received suggestions from a partner on how to strengthen your writing.

Name(s): _____

Significant Historic Events

Certain historic events are so significant that people can remember where they were and what they were doing when they happened. These events change and shape the history of our country. They have a lasting impact on what citizens believe and how they react in various situations. People should remember anniversaries of historic events so they can understand why the events are important, honor those involved, and contribute to our shared culture.

Significant historic events impact people in many different ways. A speech supporting an important cause may sway public opinion. It may result in specific action for change. Some government actions at home and abroad change the course of events that follow. Lives were lost during events such as the 9/11 attacks on the World Trade Center.

The monumental nature of such incidents often results in commemorative anniversary events. These events honor the people who were involved. For example, memorials around the country honor veterans of previous wars. A national holiday commemorates Martin Luther King's speech, among other contributions he made to society. Every year, people remember 9/11 in a variety of ways to honor innocent people who lost their lives.

The establishment of a national holiday is only one way that historic events make a difference in our shared culture. Culture is the way a group of people lives and behaves. Travelers across the country have a different experience now than they did prior to the 9/11 attacks. Another example is that President John F. Kennedy's assassination shaped future political events, such as the next election and related issues. This single event impacted not only politics but culture by making a difference in the space program and civil rights.

Discuss the following questions with your small group to plan and write a concluding paragraph for this opinion essay. Use a separate piece of paper to write the paragraph.

- What is the topic of the essay and the author's opinion about that topic?
- Which phrases or sentences will help you write a concluding paragraph?
- What is the author's purpose in the essay?
- How might the concluding paragraph reflect that purpose?
- Which technique(s) could you use to persuade readers to agree with the author's opinion?

> ### Teacher Notes
>
> Grade level: appropriate
> Lexile estimate: 990L

Name(s): _____

An Engaging Concluding Paragraph

➤ **Part One**

- Review the introductory paragraph and body paragraphs you wrote for your opinion essay in previous activities.
- Write a concluding paragraph for your essay on a separate piece of paper.

➤ **Part Two**

- Trade papers with a partner.
- Whisper-read your partner's concluding paragraph.
- Answer the following questions. Then return this page to your partner.

1. Based on this paragraph, what do you think the author is trying to say to readers in the essay?

   _____

   _____

2. What emotion do you feel after reading this paragraph? Why do you feel this way?

   _____

   _____

3. What action does the author want readers to take? How does he or she encourage readers to change their thinking or beliefs?

   _____

   _____

4. Which approach discussed during the small-group activity might be most appropriate for your partner's concluding paragraph given their topic and opinion?

   _____

   _____

5. Which feature (type of sentence) might the author add to the paragraph to engage readers?

   _____

   _____

6. What suggestion(s) would you give your partner to strengthen his or her concluding paragraph?

   _____

   _____

First Draft and Peer Review

➤ Objective

Students will use writing from previous activities in this module to write first drafts of their opinion essays. Then they will participate in a small-group peer-review activity with a specific focus for commenting on classmates' writing.

➤ Introduction

You will use your writing from previous activities in this module to write a first draft of your opinion essay. Then you will work with a small group to give and receive a review of your writing, with a specific focus.

➤ Instruction

A draft of an opinion essay will include all the parts you've worked on so far. Your draft will include an introductory paragraph. Body paragraphs will explain and support your reasons with evidence such as facts, details, and examples. Often, an opinion essay will address an opposing viewpoint to the stated opinion. This shows readers how the author's opinion is valid and worthy of readers' consideration, belief, or action. As you write your first draft, include transition words or phrases to guide readers from one paragraph to the next. The final paragraph in your essay provides a conclusion for readers and encourages them to agree with the stated opinion.

➤ Guided Practice

Refer to your notes and writing from previous activities to write a first draft of your opinion essay. Make sure your thesis statement focuses on a specific topic and clearly states your opinion. How closely do your thesis statement and the paragraphs that follow it reflect an appropriate response to the topic?

➤ Independent Practice

Agree as a class on a focus for the peer review. *For which aspect of opinion writing would you most like to receive feedback from peers? Will we focus on having a specific thesis statement that clearly gives an opinion, the appropriateness of the response to a topic, the overall effectiveness of the argument, or another area?* Distribute "A Focused Review" (page 46) and scissors. *Write the focus for review we decided on as a class. Within your small group, pass your first draft to the right. Take three minutes to read the essay and write a comment for your classmate on the first comment form. When time is up, pass the drafts to the right again to read a different classmate's essay and provide feedback.* Allow time for students to give and receive feedback for each person in their group. *Now, cut your comments apart to give each person your feedback on his or her essay.*

➤ Review

Answer any questions about specific parts of an opinion essay as students write, such as the introductory paragraph, the body paragraphs, or the concluding paragraph. Review transition words and phrases, as necessary, to assist students in writing their first drafts.

➤ Closing

You wrote a first draft of your opinion essay and received feedback from classmates. Write a quick journal entry to reflect on what you learned from the comments you received on your essay.

Name(s): _____

A Focused Review

Write the focus for review we decided on as a class.

_____

_____

Within your small group, pass your first draft to the right. Take three minutes to read the essay and write a comment for your classmate on the first comment form. When time is up, pass the drafts to the right again to read a different classmate's essay and provide feedback. Continue to comment on each classmate's essay within your group. Cut your comments apart on the dashed lines to give each person your feedback on his or her essay.

Author's Name: _____   Reader's Name: _____

Comment:

Author's Name: _____   Reader's Name: _____

Comment:

Author's Name: _____   Reader's Name: _____

Comment:

Author's Name: _____   Reader's Name: _____

Comment:

Author's Name: _____   Reader's Name: _____

Comment:

Now, write a quick journal entry to reflect on what you learned from the comments you received on your essay.

_____

_____

_____

Second Draft and Self-Evaluation

➤ Objective

Students will write a second draft of their opinion essays. Then they will collaborate to create a list of criteria describing effective opinion writing. They will compare their criteria to the characteristics described on the self-evaluation rubric and then evaluate and score their second drafts using the rubric.

➤ Introduction

You will write a second draft of your opinion essay. Then you will discuss the characteristics of effective opinion writing with classmates and create a list of criteria. You will compare your criteria with qualities of opinion writing described on a rubric and use the rubric to evaluate and score your second draft.

➤ Instruction

In the previous lesson, you worked with a small group to review your first draft. You received feedback on your essay and wrote a journal entry to reflect on what you learned about how to strengthen your writing from the comments you received from classmates. You should now have notes about things you want to change to make your writing more effective. What is the overall goal or purpose in an opinion essay? (to convince readers to change the way they think or behave) *Keep your specific purpose in mind as you revise your essay to write a second draft. Even though you have already written a rough copy of your essay, this is not your final draft. You will make more changes to this second draft.*

➤ Guided Practice

Refer to the comments you received on your first draft from classmates and to the notes you have made about things you want to change. As you write your second draft, consider who will want to read your opinion on this topic and where you might publish your writing to reach that audience.

Use an interactive whiteboard or other digital tools (e.g., class blog or a wiki) to have students work together on a collaborative shared-writing activity. *Which criteria do you think we should use to evaluate our opinion essays? Think about the characteristics of introductory paragraphs, body paragraphs, and concluding paragraphs. Contribute your ideas to the class discussion and/or post in our online (digital) format to create a list of criteria.*

➤ Independent Practice

Distribute "Self-Evaluation: Opinion Essay" (page 48). *How closely do the criteria we established for evaluating opinion essays match the descriptions of strong opinion writing on the rubric? Use the rubric to evaluate your second draft. Focus on one aspect of your essay at a time. Read that part of your writing carefully and then circle the description on the rubric that best matches your writing in that area. For each part of your essay, write one way you would like to strengthen your writing. Use the descriptions of quality writing on the rubric for ideas.*

➤ Review

Discuss the impact revising can have on the writing process. Review the categories on the rubric, discussing the qualities of writing that correspond to the scores for each category.

➤ Closing

Use the notes you made on your second draft to write a final draft of your opinion essay and bring it back to class.

Self-Evaluation: Opinion Essay

Name: _____   Score: _____

	4	3	2	1
Introductory Paragraph	My introductory paragraph begins with a sentence that captures readers' attention. It also has a thesis statement that clearly states my opinion about a current event or issue and introduces related reasons.	My introductory paragraph has a thesis statement that clearly states my opinion about a current event or issue and introduces my reasons.	My introductory paragraph includes an opinion I have about a current event or issue.	My introductory paragraph does not state an opinion and/or does not introduce any reasons.
Body Paragraphs	Each body paragraph explains and presents relevant evidence, such as facts and details, for one reason that supports my thesis statement about a current event or issue.	Each body paragraph includes a reason that supports my opinion about a current event or issue with facts and details.	Each body paragraph includes a reason and a few details about a current event or issue.	My reasons are not related to my thesis statement or the topic introduced in the introductory paragraph and do not include details.
Organization	My introductory paragraph and body paragraphs are organized in a logical way, and I use appropriate transition words and phrases.	My introductory paragraph and body paragraphs are organized, and I use some transition words and phrases.	Some of my body paragraphs are organized, but I do not use transition words and phrases.	My body paragraphs are not organized in a way that makes sense.
Concluding Paragraph	My essay has a concluding paragraph that is directly related to my thesis statement about a current event or issue and challenges readers to change the way they think or behave.	My essay has a concluding paragraph that is related to my thesis statement about a current event or issue and considers the reader's response.	My essay has a concluding paragraph that is related to my thesis statement or says something about a current event or issue.	My concluding paragraph is not related to my thesis statement and is not about a current event or issue.

Review

➤ Objective

Students will read a sample essay and answer interpretive questions. Then they will discuss the strengths and weaknesses of the essay in small groups.

➤ Introduction

You will read a sample opinion essay and answer questions about it. Then you will participate in a small-group activity to discuss the strengths and weaknesses of the essay.

➤ Instruction

Let's think about what we have learned about writing an opinion essay. Discuss. *The introductory paragraph contains a thesis statement and an overview of the reasons that support the author's opinion. Each body paragraph presents evidence, including facts and details, to support one reason. Body paragraphs should be in a logical order that relates to the overview in the introductory paragraph. A separate body paragraph may address an opposing argument. The concluding paragraph summarizes the opinion in the thesis statement and the reasons for the author's opinion. It concludes the argument and tries to convince readers the stated opinion is valid.*

➤ Guided Practice

Distribute "Delicious School Lunches" (page 50) and "Talk About the Issues" (page 51). *Sometimes a panel will discuss different perspectives on an issue before an audience. Read the sample essay about an issue and answer the questions in Part One to prepare for a small-group discussion.*

➤ Independent Practice

Divide students into small groups so that each group has at least one student who chose to represent each "role" described in the sample essay. *Appoint a "moderator" within your group to facilitate and guide the discussion. Allow each person in the group to share his or her review of the essay. As you discuss the essay and questions, consider not only the issue at hand, but also how well the essay demonstrates the qualities of effective opinion writing.*

➤ Review

Review and clarify the characteristics of effective opinion writing. Discuss students' responses on "Talk About the Issues" as necessary. As time allows, invite students to present their interpretation of the essay and its claims in a talk-show format for the class.

➤ Closing

You read and analyzed a sample opinion essay. You discussed your responses in a small group to consider how well the piece demonstrated qualities of effective opinion writing.

Name(s): _____

Delicious School Lunches

School cafeteria food takes people by surprise. One day it's great, and the next day it's salty, greasy, or just awful. Who gets to choose the food that is served at school? A committee comprised of students, parents, school administrators, and nutritionists should make decisions about food served at school.

Students should get to have a say about their lunches because they are the people who eat the food. It might be admirable for a parent or nutritionist to decide to serve vegetables, but if students won't eat them, there is a problem.

Concerned parents should also have a voice. They may repeat the quote, "You are what you eat" to make their point. If a student eats a meal lacking in balanced nutrition, he or she won't have the focus and energy needed for afternoon activities. Parents are right to have a concern for their children's well-being. For example, their children may have specific dietary needs or allergies. However, parents should also be aware that not everyone will agree on specific menu choices. Parents should keep their preferences to themselves but express their concerns.

School administrators should have representation as well. A meal might be good quality, nutritious, and delicious. However, if the price per student is too high, the school budget would limit the available choices. Administrators would help the committee make cost-efficient considerations in planning what is served in the school cafeteria.

Nutritionists would be a great resource for the committee. They would advise the group on healthy choices that meet the dietary needs of students. If a nutritionist is part of the committee, he or she could research and perform fact-finding to aid in decision-making.

We all need nutritious food for good health, energy, and focused thinking. Eating healthy food at school is good for our bodies and brains. It takes more than one person to make wise choices about the food served at school. Students should take an interest in and encourage others to learn about and participate in this vital issue.

Teacher Notes

Grade level: appropriate

Lexile estimate: 930L

Photograph by Bob Nichols/USDA (https://www.flickr.com/photos/usdagov/6276717595/), public domain image.

Name(s): _____

Talk About the Issues

➤ Part One

Read the sample essay on page 50 and write your answers to the questions on the lines.

1. What is your role in the community? _____
   _____

2. What is the topic of today's discussion? _____
   _____

3. What is the opinion expressed in the essay? _____
   _____

4. What are the reasons the author provides to support his or her opinion?
   _____
   _____

5. What relevant evidence is presented? _____
   _____

6. How is the essay organized? How does the author use transition words and phrases?
   _____
   _____

7. How does the author tie in the concluding paragraph with the thesis statement?
   _____
   _____

8. In what ways are readers challenged to change the way they think or behave?
   _____
   _____

9. What are the strengths and weaknesses of the essay? ___
   _____

10. Who would you recommend read the essay? Why? _____
    _____

➤ Part Two

- Appoint a "moderator" within your group to facilitate and guide the discussion.
- Allow each person in the group to share his or her review of the essay.
- As you discuss the essay and questions, consider not only the issue at hand, but also how well the essay demonstrates the qualities of effective opinion writing.

Final Evaluation

➤ Objective

Students will score a sample opinion essay and compare their perspectives with a think-aloud during a class discussion. They will use their observations to predict the scores they will receive on the teacher evaluations of their opinion essays and answer reflection questions.

➤ Introduction

You will use a rubric to score a sample opinion essay and then observe how I would score the same essay. You will use what you notice to predict the scores you will receive on your opinion essay and then compare your scores and your predictions with the actual scores you receive to answer reflection questions.

➤ Instruction

You evaluated your second draft using "Self-Evaluation: Opinion Essay" (page 48). This showed you characteristics of effective opinion writing I would consider when scoring your essays. The rubric gave you information to think about as you wrote your final draft. I have used a very similar rubric to score your opinion essay. We can compare scores from different sources to gain a clearer picture of strengths and weaknesses in our writing to focus on areas we would like to continue to improve.

➤ Guided Practice

Distribute "Delicious School Lunches" (page 50), "Evaluating an Opinion Essay" (page 54), and students' copies of "Self-Evaluation: Opinion Essay." *What scores would you give this essay? Use the rubric and record your scores on the chart in Part One of "Evaluating an Opinion Essay."* Discuss the strengths and weaknesses of the sample essay and model how you would use the rubric to score the writing. *Write the scores I would give the essay on the chart in Part One. How do the scores you gave the essay differ from those modeled in the class discussion? Why do you think the differences exist?* Discuss.

➤ Independent Practice

Record your scores from "Self-Evaluation: Opinion Essay" in the first column of the chart in Part Two.

Think about the differences you observed in how you scored the sample essay and how other classmates or I would score the essay. What scores do you think you will receive on your opinion essay? Write your predictions in the second column of the chart.

Distribute students' copies of "Teacher Evaluation: Opinion Essay" (page 53). *Record your scores from "Teacher Evaluation: Opinion Essay" in the last column of the chart. In what areas is your essay stronger than the model? What can you learn from evaluating the model and then reviewing the scores on your essay? What will you do differently the next time you write an opinion essay? Write your responses on a separate piece of paper.*

➤ Review

Review why different sources provide different perspectives on the same piece of writing and how these insights can help us strengthen and improve our writing.

➤ Closing

You reviewed the rubric to score a sample opinion essay and then predicted the scores your own essay would receive. You compared the scores you gave your essay with the scores you received and considered how your learning will affect your writing in the future.

Teacher Evaluation: Opinion Essay

Student Name: _____   **Score:** _____

	4	3	2	1
Introductory Paragraph	The introductory paragraph begins with a sentence that captures readers' attention. It also has a thesis statement that clearly states the author's opinion about a current event or issue and introduces related reasons.	The introductory paragraph has a thesis statement that clearly states the author's opinion about a current event or issue and introduces the author's reasons.	The introductory paragraph includes an opinion the author has about a current event or issue.	The introductory paragraph does not state an opinion and/or does not introduce any reasons.
Body Paragraphs	Each body paragraph explains and presents relevant evidence, such as facts and details, for one reason that supports the thesis statement about a current event or issue.	Each body paragraph includes a reason that supports the author's opinion about a current event or issue with facts and details.	Each body paragraph includes a reason and a few details about a current event or issue.	The author's reasons are not related to the thesis statement or the topic introduced in the introductory paragraph and do not include details.
Organization	The introductory paragraph and body paragraphs are organized in a logical way, and the author uses appropriate transition words and phrases.	The introductory paragraph and body paragraphs are organized, and the author uses some transition words and phrases.	Some of the body paragraphs are organized, but the author does not use transition words and phrases.	The body paragraphs are not organized in a way that makes sense.
Concluding Paragraph	The essay has a concluding paragraph that is directly related to the thesis statement about a current event or issue and challenges readers to change the way they think or behave.	The essay has a concluding paragraph that is related to the thesis statement about a current event or issue and considers the reader's response.	The essay has a concluding paragraph that is related to the thesis statement or says something about a current event or issue.	The concluding paragraph is not related to the thesis statement and is not about a current event or issue.

Name(s): _____

Evaluating an Opinion Essay

➤ Part One

Use the rubric to evaluate "Delicious School Lunches" (page 50). Then summarize the data below.

My Scores	Delicious School Lunches	Modeled Scores
	Introductory Paragraph	
	Body Paragraphs	
	Organization	
	Concluding Paragraph	

How do the scores you gave the essay differ from those modeled in the class discussion?

_____

_____

Why do you think the differences exist?

_____

_____

➤ Part Two

1. Record your scores from "Self-Evaluation: Opinion Essay" (page 48) in the first column of the chart below.

Self-Evaluation Scores	Predicted Teacher Scores		Actual Teacher Scores
		Introductory Paragraph	
		Body Paragraphs	
		Organization	
		Concluding Paragraph	

2. What scores do you think you will receive on your opinion essay? Write your predictions in the second column of the chart.

3. Record your scores from "Teacher Evaluation: Opinion Essay" (page 53) in the last column of the chart.

4. Answer the following questions on a separate piece of paper:
    • In what areas is your essay stronger than the model?
    • What can you learn from evaluating the model and then reviewing the scores on your essay?
    • What will you do differently the next time you write an opinion essay?

All About Informative/Explanatory Writing

➤ Objective

Students will read and analyze sample paragraphs to identify characteristics of informative writing. They will also modify a paragraph and then discuss with partners what specific aspects of informative writing contribute to a piece as a whole.

➤ Introduction

Today you will read and analyze sample paragraphs to learn about characteristics of effective informative writing. You will also modify a sample and then discuss with a partner how the characteristics of informative writing work together as a whole to make a paragraph effective. Our topic for this module is online communities.

➤ Instruction

Informative writing examines a topic to convey ideas and information. Explanatory writing explains how something works or tells readers how to do something. This type of writing tells how or why. It may define, describe, or explain the topic. A topic sentence clearly introduces what the paragraph will be about. It explains information clearly so readers can understand the topic. Information is grouped in a way that makes sense. Facts, definitions, details, and examples explain the topic for readers. A concluding sentence relates to the topic and restates the main idea.

➤ Guided Practice

Display "Social Media and Online Communities" (page 56, strong example), covering up the Teacher Notes, and distribute "Analyze an Informative Paragraph" (page 58). *How does this paragraph demonstrate the characteristics of informative writing?* Display "What Is an Online Community?" (page 57, weak example), covering up the Teacher Notes. *Answer the questions in Part One for each paragraph. How does the second paragraph compare to the first paragraph we analyzed? Which paragraph is more effective? Why?*

➤ Independent Practice

Distribute "A Safe Online Experience" (page 59, strong example) to half of the class and "Online Communities for Everyone" (page 60, weak example) to the other half of the class. *Rewrite your assigned paragraph on a separate piece of paper, leaving out one aspect of an informative paragraph. For example, you can omit the topic sentence, a key detail, an explanation, or the concluding sentence, or change the organizational structure. Trade papers with a partner and identify which aspect your partner changed or removed in his or her assigned paragraph. What is missing from the paragraph? What would the missing phrase or sentence contribute to the paragraph? Use the questions in Part One to discuss each of your assigned paragraphs with your partner.*

➤ Review

Review students' responses to the questions in Part Two of "Analyze an Informative Paragraph" to answer questions and clarify what each characteristic of informative writing contributes to a piece as a whole.

➤ Closing

You read and analyzed examples of informative writing to identify specific characteristics and how they contribute to an effective informative piece.

Social Media and Online Communities

In this digital age, many people interact more online than they do in person. Parents and other concerned adults question how healthy this is for students. Social media has risks as well as benefits. Through online communities, youth run the risk of being exposed to cyberbullying and predators. Some children use cellphones or social media to connect with friends. They do not meet face to face, such as going to the mall or to someone's house, as often. Students who participate in social media may have trouble managing their time wisely. On the other hand, social media and online communities help children learn communication skills. They develop these skills through written and technical avenues, which will provide them with some essential life skills. Online communities provide students with the opportunity to interact with others and to form a sense of identity. Social media engages children with different learning styles. As long as children become involved with others in a variety of ways, online communities and social media can provide a healthy avenue for learning social skills.

Teacher Notes

This paragraph is a <u>strong</u> example of informative writing for these reasons:

- The topic sentence introduces the topic: *people interact more online than they do in person.*
- This informative paragraph describes and explains the topic of online interaction.
- Information is grouped in a way that makes sense: first the risks are discussed, then the benefits of social media are described.
- Details and examples explain information about the topic for readers.
- The concluding sentence summarizes the topic of online interaction with other people.

> Grade level: appropriate
> Lexile estimate: 1020L

What Is an Online Community?

Online communities are virtual communities where people interact with others on the Internet. One kind of electronic communication is social media. People communicate online through email, blogs, or online forums. They may use websites such as Facebook or Twitter. On these sites and others, users create virtual communities to share information, ideas, and personal messages. Often, participants in

an online community share one or more common interests. In order to be part of an online community, users need an Internet connection and a device to access and update their profiles. In this digital age, the majority of people who have an Internet connection are part of at least one online community.

Teacher Notes

This paragraph is a <u>weak</u> example of informative writing for the following reasons:

- The topic sentence is vague.
- Some details are irrelevant. (e.g., "One kind of electronic communication is social media.")
- Some of the information is not arranged in a way that makes sense.
- The concluding sentence refers back to the topic but does not summarize the information presented.

> Grade level: appropriate
> Lexile estimate: 1040L

Name(s): _____

Analyze an Informative Paragraph

➤ Part One

Read the paragraphs displayed in class (A—"Social Media and Online Communities" [page 56] and B—"What Is an Online Community?" [page 57]) and answer the questions below to think about how each piece demonstrates characteristics of effective informative writing.

1. What is the main idea of the paragraph?

A. _____

B. _____

2. What is the author's purpose in writing this paragraph? How well does he or she accomplish this purpose?

A. _____

B. _____

3. What details and evidence develop the main idea?

A. _____

B. _____

4. How is information in the paragraph organized?

A. _____

B. _____

5. How does the concluding sentence summarize the topic?

A. _____

B. _____

6. What is one strength of the paragraph?

A. _____

B. _____

7. What would you change to strengthen the writing?

A. _____

B. _____

➤ Part Two

- Rewrite your assigned paragraph ("A Safe Online Experience" or "Online Communities for Everyone") on a separate piece of paper, leaving out one aspect of an informative paragraph. For example, you can omit the topic sentence, a key detail, an explanation, or the concluding sentence, or change the organizational structure.
- Trade papers with a partner.
- Identify which aspect your partner changed or removed in his or her assigned paragraph. Discuss how the missing component would contribute to the paragraph.
- Use the questions in Part One to discuss each of your assigned paragraphs with your partner.

A Safe Online Experience

Students can reap benefits and avoid the dangers of social media by putting safe practices in place.

Talk with grownups to establish an environment of trust. This creates a place to ask questions and

deal with various online issues that arise. As a family, it is wise to develop guidelines for the amount of

acceptable social media use. This holds all family members accountable to one another for their online

behavior. Parents and children can talk with one another about integrity, social skills, and privacy

issues. Include guidelines for supervision as part of a family plan. Supervision protects youth and

enables them to enjoy their experiences in online communities and stay safe at the same time. Not

only do these discussions keep children safe, limits on social media use help them stay healthy. Often

users get caught up in an online experience. Social media may interfere with sleep, physical activity,

and schoolwork. Accountability and safe Internet practices enable children to stay healthy by setting

limits on how often they use social media and which type they use.

Teacher Notes

Grade level: appropriate
Lexile estimate: 1030L

Online Communities for Everyone

Online communities bring people together for a variety of purposes. Some communities offer a forum for people with common interests to communicate with one another. The purpose may be as simple as participating in a discussion about a specific topic. It may be more complex, with members sharing experiences or information to help each other with tasks or problems. Other online communities use data from each individual to help make the whole community more helpful to the users. One example is Netflix, an online video-streaming service. Members allow Netflix to gather information about the movies and TV shows they watch. In return, Netflix offers suggestions

based on the viewing habits of others who have watched those same films or shows. By using data from each individual, Netflix can create a custom experience for you. Children may join a gaming community. Often, players work together to accomplish various goals. The variety and specific purposes of online communities demonstrate their place in society.

Teacher Notes

Grade level: appropriate
Lexile estimate: 960L

Topic Sentences

➤ Objective

Students will exchange ideas with classmates to brainstorm possible topics for their informative paragraphs. They will then note areas in which they will need to research to learn more about their topics. Students will also practice writing different types of topic sentences to explore ways they can introduce their topics.

➤ Introduction

You will exchange ideas about the general topic for this module with classmates to brainstorm a specific topic and focus for your informative paragraph. This will help you identify areas in which you will need to research and gather information. Then you will practice writing different types of topic sentences to introduce what your paragraph will be about.

➤ Instruction

The topic sentence clearly states the main idea of an informative paragraph. It gives readers an idea of the information they will read about. The subject must be specific enough to discuss in one paragraph. The topic sentence should have a particular focus. This lets readers know how you will approach the topic. For example, will your paragraph define, describe, or explain? State the topic in an interesting way, so readers will want to continue reading the paragraph.

➤ Guided Practice

Before you write a topic sentence for your informative paragraph, you'll need to decide on a specific topic. Our topic for this module is online communities. Which particular aspect of this topic will you describe or explain to your readers? What unique perspective or information do you have to offer? Distribute "An Exchange of Ideas" (page 62). *Brainstorm with classmates by talking with one person at a time to exchange ideas about how you can narrow your focus to write about this topic. Then answer the questions in Part Two.*

➤ Independent Practice

Distribute "Introduce Your Topic" (page 63). *When we interact with others in a community, often we introduce what we want to talk about. There are different ways we do this, without even thinking about it. In the same way, there are different types of topic sentences we can use to introduce what a paragraph will be about. Follow the suggestion in each speech bubble to write sample topic sentences that introduce the topic of your informative paragraph.*

➤ Review

Model or provide examples of different types of topic sentences as suggested on "Introduce Your Topic." As time allows, invite students to share their samples and discuss what makes an effective topic sentence that would engage readers.

➤ Closing

You brainstormed topic ideas for your informative paragraph and made notes about the research you will do to gather information about your chosen topic. You also wrote different types of sample topic sentences.

Name(s): _____

An Exchange of Ideas

➤ Part One

Brainstorm with classmates to explore how you can narrow your focus about the general topic:
online communities. Which particular aspect of this topic could you describe or explain to readers?
What unique perspective, knowledge, or information do you have to offer?

1. Write one idea you have in the first row of the left column.

2. Talk with a classmate to share ideas. Write your classmate's idea in the right column.

3. Now that you have started to think and talk about the topic, write another idea you have in
    the second row of the left column.

4. Share this new idea with a different classmate and write his or her idea in the right column.

5. Continue this process to complete the chart.

My Idea	A Classmate's Idea

➤ Part Two

Review the ideas you have and comments you received from classmates. Then answer the question:
what will be the topic of your informative paragraph?

_____

_____

What key words, phrases, or questions will you need to research to gather information for your topic?

```



```

Name(s): _____

Introduce Your Topic

The speech bubbles below describe different types of topic sentences. Follow the suggestion in each bubble to write sample topic sentences that introduce the topic of your informative paragraph.

Ask a question.

Capture a moment.

Begin with a quotation.

Use a sensory detail.

Introduce an interesting or unusual fact.

Paint a picture for readers.

Make a personal connection with the topic.

Write a preview leading into the paragraph details about the topic.

Supporting Details

➤ Objective

Students will research their topics and complete charts with bibliographic information. Then they will identify specific details to include in their informative paragraphs and decide on an organizational structure for their writing. They will also discuss with partners how they can use elements of style to accomplish their purpose and engage readers.

➤ Introduction

You will research information about your topic and take notes on a chart. Then you will identify specific details to include in your paragraph and decide on an organizational structure for your writing. You will also discuss how to use word choice and sentence structure in your writing to engage readers.

➤ Instruction

Supporting details help readers better understand the topic. This information may include facts, definitions, concrete details, quotations, or examples related to the topic. Group details together to emphasize each point you want to make about the topic. Use concrete nouns and vivid verbs to create a mental picture for your reader. Define any words specific to your topic that might be unfamiliar to readers.

➤ Guided Practice

Distribute "Facts & Details" (page 65). *Review your topic and ideas for research from "An Exchange of Ideas" (page 62). Think about the main idea you want to explore and your reason for writing about this topic. Write your answers to the first two questions in the appropriate columns of the chart. Use available print and online resources to research information about your topic. Write notes from your research in the appropriate columns of the chart. Include bibliographic information about each source.*

Distribute "Specific Details" (page 66). *Review your notes from "Facts & Details" to identify specific information you will include in your paragraph. Write an example of each type of detail that would be appropriate for your topic. Then think about the best way to organize your information for readers. Read the list of ways to organize information in Part Two. Draw a star by the organizational structure you plan to use for your paragraph.*

➤ Independent Practice

Distribute "Connect with Your Audience" (page 67). *Each online community has its own personality or style for a unique purpose, audience, and context. What is the purpose of your informative paragraph? Who is your specific audience? Use your notes from "Facts & Details" and "Specific Details" to write sentences for your informative paragraph. Trade papers with a partner and review his or her answers and sentences in Part One. Then answer the questions in Part Two about his or her writing.*

➤ Review

Review the format for bibliographic information you wish students to use and model a sample bibliographic entry as time allows. Display sample informative paragraphs to discuss how authors use word choice and sentence structure to accomplish their purpose and engage readers.

➤ Closing

You researched the topic of your informative paragraph and took notes. Then you focused on specific details and thought about the best way to organize your information. You also gave and received input from a partner about your writing.

Name(s): _____

Facts & Details

Review your topic and ideas for research from "An Exchange of Ideas" (page 62). Think about the main idea you want to explore and your reason for writing about this topic.

- What do you already know about your topic?
- What do you want to research and learn more about?

Use available print and online resources to research information about your topic.

- What did you learn?
- Which sources did you use for each fact or detail?

What I Know	What I Want to Learn	What I Learned	My Sources

Name(s): _____

Specific Details

➤ Part One

Review your notes from "Facts & Details" (page 65) to identify specific information you will include in your paragraph.

Fact	Definition
One relevant fact about my topic is . . .	One word related to my topic that readers might need defined is . . .

Detail	Example
One detail that further describes or explains my topic for readers is . . .	One example that helps explain my topic is . . .

Quotation
One quotation from an expert that might add interest to my paragraph is . . .

➤ Part Two

Review what you have learned from researching your topic. Which would be the best way to present your information to readers? Draw a star by the organizational structure you plan to use for your paragraph.

☐ Describe and define   ☐ Compare and contrast   ☐ Explain how something works

☐ Group related ideas   ☐ Show cause and effect

Name(s): _____

Connect with Your Audience

➤ Part One

Each online community has its own personality or style for a unique purpose, audience, and context.

- What is the purpose of your informative paragraph?

  _____

- Who is your specific audience?

  _____

Use your notes from "Facts & Details" (page 65) and "Specific Details" (page 66) to write sentences for your informative paragraph.

_____

_____

_____

_____

_____

_____

_____

_____

➤ Part Two

Trade papers with a partner and review his or her answers and sentences in Part One. Then answer the questions below about his or her writing.

- How does the author's choice of words accomplish his or her purpose?

  _____

  _____

- Which precise words and descriptions engage readers?

  _____

  _____

- How will the sentence structure and fluency appeal to a specific audience?

  _____

  _____

Transition Words

➤ Objective

Students will write sentences from their paragraphs and add appropriate transition words and phrases. They will then discuss their writing with partners and revise their sentences as needed.

➤ Introduction

You will write sentences from your paragraph on a graphic organizer. Then you will add transition words and phrases to connect your ideas in a logical way and discuss your writing with a partner.

➤ Instruction

Authors use transition words to connect sentences and ideas to guide readers through text. These words connect the main idea of an informative paragraph with the details and explanations. Transition words establish relationships between thoughts and ideas within the paragraph. In an informative paragraph, the most important ideas or details may be first or last. Transition words have various purposes. They may show location or time. Transition words can add information or emphasize a point. Other words or phrases compare or contrast concepts. Not all sentences need a transition word.

➤ Guided Practice

Distribute "Connected Ideas" (page 69) and highlighters. *Just as people make connections with others in online communities, authors use transition words and phrases to make connections between ideas in their writing. Refer to "Connect with Your Audience" (page 67) to write sentences from your paragraph in the boxes. Write additional sentences, as needed, to form complete thoughts. Use transition words from the cloud to connect your ideas in a way that makes sense. Write the transition words on the lines connecting the boxes. Highlight any transition words or phrases you used within your sentences as well.*

➤ Independent Practice

Work with a partner to identify and suggest appropriate transition words for your sentences. You may find your writing works better with a word not listed in the word cloud. Revise your writing, as needed, to make connections between sentences to clarify your ideas for readers.

➤ Review

Review examples of how authors use transition words in informative paragraphs from available resources and sample paragraphs. As time allows, create a class chart or list to expand on the transition words and phrases suggested on "Connected Ideas" for student reference.

➤ Closing

You referred to a list of suggested transition words and phrases to include transitions in the sentences you wrote for your informative paragraph. You gave and received feedback from a partner to revise your sentences to use transitions appropriately.

Name(s): _____

Connected Ideas

Just as people make connections with others in online communities, authors use transition words and phrases to make connections between ideas in their writing.

1. Refer to "Connect with Your Audience" (page 67) to write sentences from your paragraph in the boxes. Write additional sentences, as needed, to form complete thoughts.

2. Use transition words from the cloud below to connect your ideas in a way that makes sense. Write the transition words on the lines connecting the boxes.

3. Highlight any transition words or phrases you used within your sentences.

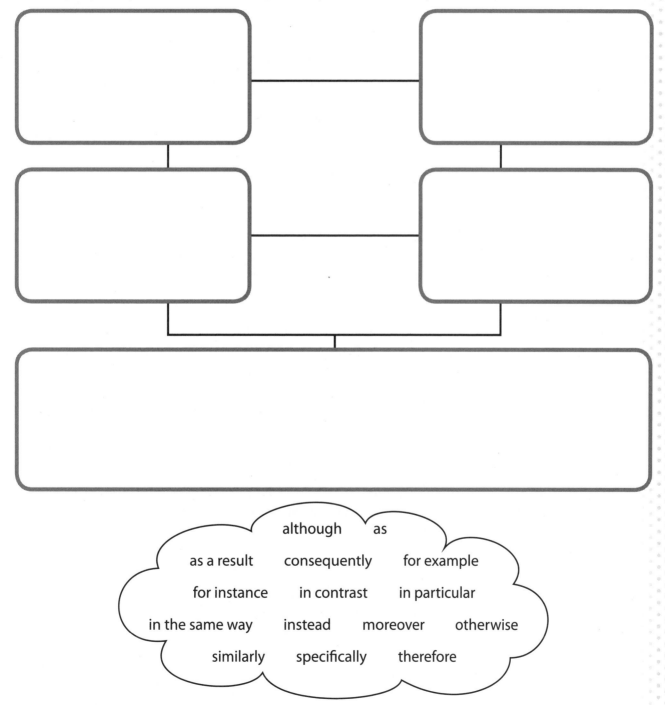

Concluding Sentences

➤ Objective

Students will write concluding sentences for a sample informative paragraph. They will share their sentences with classmates and discuss the effectiveness of different types of concluding sentences represented. Then students will consider reflection questions to write concluding sentences for their own paragraphs.

➤ Introduction

You will write a concluding sentence for a sample informative paragraph and discuss different types of concluding sentences with classmates. Then you will read questions to reflect on your paragraph and write a concluding sentence.

➤ Instruction

The concluding sentence of an informative paragraph relates to the information in the paragraph. It restates the topic sentence in different words and summarizes the main idea. The concluding sentence may emphasize the importance of the topic for readers or leave them with a thought for reflection. A concluding sentence in an informative paragraph may ask a question for readers to consider or suggest that readers take action based on the information presented. A strong concluding sentence gives readers a sense that the paragraph is finished. If your paragraph explains parts of something or provides examples, the concluding sentence should tie it all together.

➤ Guided Practice

Distribute "A Strong Concluding Sentence" (page 71). *Complete Part One by writing and sharing a concluding sentence for the informative paragraph.* Display anonymous student-generated concluding sentences for the paragraph. *Which types of concluding sentences did your classmates write? Which type(s) of concluding sentences would be most effective for this paragraph? Why?*

➤ Independent Practice

Reflect on the questions in Part Two to think about a concluding sentence for your own informative paragraph. Which details in your paragraph support your topic sentence? What can you emphasize about your topic in your concluding sentence based on the examples described in the paragraph? What suggestion could you make to readers based on the information presented? What is one conclusion about the topic readers might draw based on the information in the paragraph? Review the sentences you wrote for your paragraph on "Connected Ideas" (page 69). Then write a concluding sentence for your informative paragraph.

➤ Review

Review the types of concluding sentences and discuss their use and effectiveness for informative paragraphs. Provide additional examples from classroom resources if possible. Review the reflection questions and use the sample paragraph on "A Strong Concluding Sentence" to think aloud and model writing a concluding sentence.

➤ Closing

You read a sample informative paragraph, wrote a concluding sentence, and discussed classmates' examples. Then you considered the topic and information presented in your own paragraph and wrote a concluding sentence.

Name(s): _____

A Strong Concluding Sentence

➤ Part One

Read the informative paragraph below, and then write a concluding sentence for it. Share your concluding sentence with a small group.

Online Community Technology

It takes technology to host and run an online community. People use social-media apps to access information from different devices, including cellphones. People should be able to log on to the community with email on the website or on a mobile app. Most social-media platforms do not require downloading a program onto a computer. The platform should allow people to communicate, share, and learn from one another. Some sites permit members to form groups within the social-media platform. Most offer a search feature, so users can search for members of the community. They may not be searching by name but by interests or other general categories of information.

Teacher Notes
Grade level: below
Lexile estimate: 890L

Write a concluding sentence for the informative paragraph. Then share your sentence with a small group.

_____

_____

➤ Part Two

Reflect on the following questions to think about a concluding sentence for your own informative paragraph.

- Which details in your paragraph support your topic sentence?
- What can you emphasize about your topic in your concluding sentence based on the examples described in the paragraph?
- What suggestion could you make to readers based on the information presented?
- What is one conclusion about the topic readers might draw based on the information in the paragraph?

Review the sentences you wrote for your paragraph on "Connected Ideas" (page 69). Then write a concluding sentence for your informative paragraph on the lines below.

_____

_____

_____

First Draft and Peer Review

➤ Objective

Students will write first drafts of their informative paragraphs and review the characteristics of effective informative writing. They will participate in a peer-review activity to consider their writing goals and evaluate their first drafts.

➤ Introduction

You will use your writing from previous activities in this module to write a first draft of your informative paragraph. Then you will use a list of characteristics of informative writing to evaluate a classmate's writing and review your own writing goals.

➤ Instruction

When you write a first draft, you write sentences about all your ideas. This is when you start to bring together your thoughts and notes about your topic. In the process, you may discover you need more information about something you want to say. In a first draft, crossing out text and making notes in the margins is acceptable and expected. First drafts are also called rough drafts: they are messy, and that's okay.

➤ Guided Practice

Provide guidance, as needed, as students write their first drafts. *Write the topic sentence that best fits the topic, purpose, and focus of your paragraph from "Introduce Your Topic" (page 63). Remember to use the organizational structure you chose on "Specific Details" (page 66). Refer to the sample sentences you wrote on "Connect with Your Audience" (page 67) and "Connected Ideas" (page 69). Make sure you use any revised versions of your sentences. Copy your concluding sentence from "A Strong Concluding Sentence" (page 71).*

Discuss positive ways to comment on classmates' writing. *A balanced, constructive review includes a compliment, suggestions, and an idea for strengthening the writing.*

➤ Independent Practice

Distribute "Moving Toward Excellence" (page 73). *Answer the questions in boxes 1 and 2 on a separate piece of paper. Meet with a partner to discuss the criteria you will use to review your writing. Trade first drafts with your partner and read your partner's informative paragraph. Refer to the criteria you discussed to write comments about your partner's writing on a piece of paper. Exchange papers and read the comments your partner wrote about your paragraph. Then answer the questions in boxes 3 and 4 on the same paper you used to answer questions 1 and 2.*

➤ Review

Review the importance of setting goals for writing, using criteria to evaluate progress in meeting those goals, revising, and setting new goals for continued improvement in writing.

➤ Closing

You wrote a first draft of your informative paragraph and reviewed the characteristics of effective informative writing. Then you evaluated a classmate's writing and considered your own writing progress.

Name(s): _____

Moving Toward Excellence

1. On a separate piece of paper, answer the questions in boxes 1 and 2 below.

2. Meet with a partner to discuss how you will use the following criteria to review your writing:

   - The paragraph introduces a topic in an interesting way with a clear topic sentence.
   - Related information and ideas in the paragraph are organized in a logical way to emphasize specific points about the topic.
   - The paragraph has facts, definitions, concrete details, and examples that clearly develop the topic.
   - Transition words connect sentences and ideas back to the main idea of the paragraph.
   - The paragraph has a concluding sentence that summarizes the information and restates the main idea.
   - The sentences are complete, and there are very few errors in grammar, word usage, capitalization, punctuation, and spelling.

3. Trade first drafts with your partner and read your partner's informative paragraph.

4. Write comments about your partner's writing on a separate piece of paper.

5. Exchange papers and read the comments your partner wrote about your paragraph.

6. Then answer the questions in boxes 3 and 4 on the same piece of paper you used to answer questions 1 and 2.

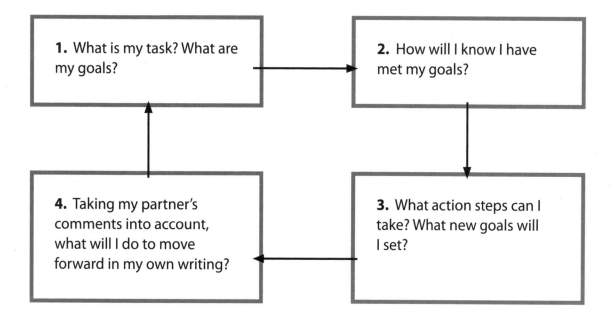

Second Draft and Self-Evaluation

➤ Objective

Students will write second drafts of their informative paragraphs and use a rubric to evaluate and score their writing. Then they will answer and discuss response questions about a self-evaluation.

➤ Introduction

You will refer to your revision notes from a previous lesson to write a second draft of your informative paragraph. Then you will use a rubric to evaluate your writing and discuss your experience with classmates in a small group.

➤ Instruction

When we evaluate our writing, we look closely at it. We can ask questions and use a rubric to guide our revision process. A rubric is a learning tool. It shows the characteristics of effective informative writing. We can focus on a specific aspect and think about how we are doing in meeting these goals in our writing. Key words and phrases in a rubric can help us identify strengths and weaknesses in our writing.

➤ Guided Practice

What is the purpose of informative writing? (to examine a topic and convey ideas and information clearly) *How do we know whether our writing meets this purpose?* Discuss. Distribute "Self-Evaluation: Informative Paragraph" (page 75) and different-colored highlighters. *Keep the key words and phrases that describe effective informative writing on the rubric in mind and use your notes on "Moving Toward Excellence" (page 73) to write a second draft of your informative paragraph.*

➤ Independent Practice

Focus on one category at a time to evaluate your writing. Read the description for each score or level of quality of writing. Choose a color to represent strengths in your writing. Highlight key words and phrases in the column for a score of "4" that match specific areas of your writing to show your strengths. Choose a different color to represent areas you would like to improve in your writing. Highlight key words to remind you about things you would like to work on in your writing.

Now look at each category again and read the descriptions for each level of quality of writing. Circle the description for the score that best matches your writing for that part of your paragraph.

Distribute "Evaluating My Writing" (page 76). *Review the scores you gave your writing on "Self-Evaluation: Informative Paragraph." Write your responses to the questions on the lines. Then work with a small group to discuss the process of evaluating your writing.*

➤ Review

Review the importance of evaluating and revising writing using a rubric as a tool. Go over specific aspects of conventions, as necessary, to assist students with that part of their evaluation.

➤ Closing

You wrote a second draft of your informative paragraph and used a rubric to evaluate your writing for strengths and weaknesses. Then you discussed response questions with a small group.

Self-Evaluation: Informative Paragraph

Name: _____   Score: _____

	4	3	2	1
Topic Sentence	My paragraph introduces a topic about online communities in an interesting way. It has a clear topic sentence.	My paragraph has a clear topic sentence about online communities.	The topic of online communities is mentioned in my paragraph.	It is unclear whether my paragraph is about online communities.
Organization	Related information and ideas in my paragraph are organized in a logical way to emphasize specific points about my topic.	Related information and ideas are grouped together in a way that makes sense.	Some information and ideas are grouped together.	Information and ideas are not organized in a way that makes sense.
Supporting Details	My paragraph has facts, definitions, concrete details, and examples that clearly develop my topic about online communities.	My paragraph has facts, definitions, details, and examples about online communities.	My paragraph has some details, such as facts, definitions, or examples, about online communities.	My paragraph does not have many details about online communities.
Transition Words	I use a variety of transition words to connect my sentences and ideas back to the main idea of my paragraph.	I use transition words to connect ideas within my paragraph.	I use at least one transition word to connect ideas within my paragraph.	I do not use any transition words to connect ideas.
Concluding Sentence	My paragraph has a concluding sentence that summarizes the information or restates my main idea about online communities.	My paragraph has a concluding sentence that closely relates to my main idea about online communities.	My paragraph has a concluding sentence about online communities.	My paragraph does not have a clear concluding sentence, or the concluding sentence is not about online communities.
Conventions	My sentences are complete, and I have very few errors in grammar, word usage, capitalization, punctuation, and spelling.	Most of my sentences are complete. Any errors in grammar, word usage, capitalization, punctuation, or spelling do not affect the meaning of my writing.	Some of my sentences are incomplete. There are errors in grammar, word usage, capitalization, punctuation, or spelling that make my writing hard to read and understand.	Many of my sentences are incomplete. There are many errors in grammar, word usage, capitalization, punctuation, or spelling that make my writing hard to read and understand.

Name(s): _____

Evaluating My Writing

Review the scores you gave your writing on "Self-Evaluation: Informative Paragraph" (page 75). Write your responses to the questions on the lines below. Then work with a small group to discuss the process of evaluating your writing.

1. How would you rate your objectivity in evaluating your writing?

_____

_____

2. What makes evaluating your own writing easy or difficult?

_____

_____

3. How does using a rubric help you evaluate your writing?

_____

_____

4. What is the greatest strength of your paragraph?

_____

_____

5. What is a weakness of your paragraph?

_____

_____

Now, work with a small group to discuss the process of evaluating your writing.

- Discuss your answer to the first question with the person on your right.
- Turn and discuss your answer to the second question with the person on your left.
- Refer to your response to the third question to talk with your group about what it means to use a rubric to evaluate writing.
- Review your answer to the fourth question. Share a strength of your paragraph with one person in your group.
- Review your answer to the fifth question. Share with a different person in your group a weakness in your writing and how you plan to strengthen it.

Final Draft

➤ Objective

Students will discuss and consider illustrations to enhance their topics for readers. Then they will use revision notes to write a final draft of their informative paragraphs. They will reflect on their roles as writers and brainstorm potential audiences for their writing.

➤ Introduction

Today you will think about appropriate illustrations for your informative paragraph. Then you will use your revision notes from a previous lesson to write a final draft. You will also identify your potential audience and your role as a writer in writing this piece.

➤ Instruction

A final draft is as correct as possible; words and sentences are capitalized correctly and have correct spelling, punctuation, and grammar. Sometimes informative or explanatory text has illustrations to help readers understand the content. Illustrations may include a chart, diagram, or map. The author has reviewed the information to make sure it is organized as logically as possible to develop the topic.

➤ Guided Practice

We can think about our audience to determine the best illustrations, if any, to include with our informative paragraph. Who would be most interested in reading about your topic? What do those readers need to know? What text features would add to your description or explanation to increase reader understanding? Display sample nonfiction text features, such as headings, photographs with captions, drawings, charts, diagrams, or maps. Discuss how specific features might add to informative writing, for example, one of the sample paragraphs from Day 1.

Refer to any revision notes on your second draft and your notes from "Evaluating My Writing" (page 76) to write a final draft of your informative paragraph.

➤ Independent Practice

Distribute "Writers and Readers" (page 78). *Which of the following author roles do you most identify with in writing your informative paragraph? Circle the cap that describes your role as a writer. Reflect on the topic of your informative paragraph and consider your audience. On each cap, write a person or group of people who will want to read your writing.* Ask each student in turn to share. *How will you fulfill the role of writer with your final draft?* Allow students who are unsure of an answer to "pass." Go around the class again, asking students in turn to share. *What is one potential audience for your writing? Why will this audience be interested in reading about your topic?* As time allows, return to students who "passed" to give them another opportunity to share.

➤ Review

Provide resources and assistance as students plan and prepare any illustrations for their final drafts. Provide technology resources for students to produce their final copies.

➤ Closing

You used technology to produce a final copy of your informative paragraph, including any appropriate illustrations. You considered your role as a writer and identified a potential audience for your writing.

Name(s): _____

Writers and Readers

1. Which of the following author roles do you most identify with in writing your informative paragraph? Circle the cap that describes your role as a writer.

    I communicate ideas and information effectively to readers.

    I provide a clear path through my writing for readers to follow.

    I express my purpose in writing and understanding of the topic.

    I communicate what I have learned about the topic in a way that makes it relevant for readers.

2. Reflect on the topic of your informative paragraph and consider your audience.
    *   Who will want to read your writing?
    *   Who is your audience?
    *   Why will these people want to read about it?
    *   In what ways might your topic and writing be relevant for your audience?

3. On each cap, write a person or group of people who will want to read your writing.

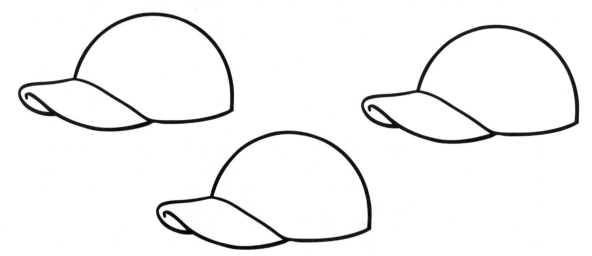

4. Share with classmates one way in which you will fulfill the role of a writer with the final draft of your informative paragraph.

5. Share with classmates one potential audience for your writing and why this audience would be interested in reading about your topic.

Final Evaluation

➤ Objective

Students will review and graph the scores from their self-evaluations on line graphs. They will then plot the scores their writing received from the teacher. They will answer questions to reflect on their progress in meeting characteristics of effective informative writing.

➤ Introduction

You will review the scores you gave your informative writing and plot your scores on a line graph. Then you will plot the scores you received from me on a teacher evaluation. You will answer questions to observe and reflect on your interpretation of the data on the graph.

➤ Instruction

In a previous lesson, you completed a self-evaluation activity in which you used a rubric to score your informative paragraphs. We use rubrics as learning tools to measure and analyze progress and improvement in specific areas. The informative paragraph rubric describes the characteristics of informative writing. How would you summarize or describe effective informative writing in one sentence? (It examines a topic and conveys ideas and information clearly.) *We can use a line graph to assess change and progress over a period of time.*

➤ Guided Practice

Distribute various colored pencils, "Graphing My Progress" (page 81), and students' copies of "Student Evaluation: Informative Paragraph" (page 75) and "Teacher Evaluation: Informative Paragraph" (page 80). *Plot the scores you gave your writing on "Self-Evaluation: Informative Paragraph" on the line graph. Use a different color to plot the scores you received on "Teacher Evaluation: Informative Paragraph" on the line graph. How closely do your scores match? Many of the scores may be similar. This may show you an overview of the quality of your writing. It can also indicate areas in which you and the teacher agree on the characteristics of your writing. One or two scores may be very different. You may want to look closely at the area represented by the different score and ask yourself why the difference exists. Is this area a particular strength, something you know how to do well? Is this an area that needs focused attention for improvement?*

➤ Independent Practice

Answer the questions to reflect on your progress in informative writing. In what areas are you making progress toward meeting the characteristics of effective informative writing? Review the goals you set on "Moving Toward Excellence" (page 73). How well are you doing at making progress toward meeting your goals for strengthening your writing?

➤ Review

Review how to plot points on a line graph and interpret data as necessary. Clarify and answer any questions students have about the teacher evaluations.

➤ Closing

You graphed scores from a self-evaluation and a teacher evaluation on a line graph. Then you answered questions to reflect on your progress in writing an informative paragraph.

Teacher Evaluation: Informative Paragraph

Student Name: _____ **Score:** _____

	4	3	2	1
Topic Sentence	The paragraph introduces a topic about online communities in an interesting way. It has a clear topic sentence.	The paragraph has a clear topic sentence about online communities.	The topic of online communities is mentioned in the paragraph.	It is unclear whether the paragraph is about online communities.
Organization	Related information and ideas in the paragraph are organized in a logical way to emphasize specific points about the topic.	Related information and ideas are grouped together in a way that makes sense.	Some information and ideas are grouped together.	Information and ideas are not organized in a way that makes sense.
Supporting Details	The paragraph has facts, definitions, concrete details, and examples that clearly develop the topic about online communities.	The paragraph has facts, definitions, details, and examples about online communities.	The paragraph has some details, such as facts, definitions, or examples, about online communities.	The paragraph does not have many details about online communities.
Transition Words	The author uses a variety of transition words to connect sentences and ideas back to the main idea of the paragraph.	The author uses transition words to connect ideas within the paragraph.	The author uses at least one transition word to connect ideas within the paragraph.	The author does not use any transition words to connect ideas.
Concluding Sentence	The paragraph has a concluding sentence that summarizes the information or restates the main idea about online communities.	The paragraph has a concluding sentence that closely relates to the main idea about online communities.	The paragraph has a concluding sentence about online communities.	The paragraph does not have a clear concluding sentence, or the concluding sentence is not about online communities.
Conventions	Sentences are complete, and there are very few errors in grammar, word usage, capitalization, punctuation, and spelling.	Most sentences are complete. Any errors in grammar, word usage, capitalization, punctuation, or spelling do not affect the meaning of the writing.	Some sentences are incomplete. There are errors in grammar, word usage, capitalization, punctuation, or spelling that make the writing hard to read and understand.	Many sentences are incomplete. There are many errors in grammar, word usage, capitalization, punctuation, or spelling that make the writing hard to read and understand.

Name(s): _____

Graphing My Progress

A line graph provides an opportunity to view change across a period of time. Create a line graph to show how your writing has improved during this module.

1. Plot the scores you gave your writing on "Self-Evaluation: Informative Paragraph" (page 75) on the line graph below.

2. Use a different color to plot the scores you received on "Teacher Evaluation: Informative Paragraph" (page 80) on the line graph.

4					
3					
2					
1					

Topic Sentence   **Organization**   **Supporting Details**   **Transition Words**   **Concluding Sentence**   **Conventions**

3. How would you compare your scores? How closely do your scores match?

    _____

    _____

    _____

    _____

4. In what areas are you making progress toward meeting the characteristics of effective informative writing?

    _____

    _____

    _____

    _____

5. Review the goals you set on "Moving Toward Excellence" (page 73). How well are you doing at making progress toward meeting your goals for strengthening your writing?

    _____

    _____

    _____

    _____

Review

➤ Objective

Students will read and evaluate a sample informative paragraph using a rubric. Then they will identify and mark characteristics of informative writing in the paragraph and complete sentence prompts.

➤ Introduction

You will work with a small group to read and evaluate a sample informative paragraph using a rubric. Then you will identify and mark characteristics of informative writing in the paragraph and complete sentence prompts. You will discuss your observations with a partner.

➤ Instruction

We have been learning about informative and explanatory writing, and you have written an informative paragraph. You have studied characteristics of informative writing and used a rubric to evaluate your writing. In this lesson, you will use a similar rubric to evaluate a sample informative paragraph.

➤ Guided Practice

Distribute unmarked copies of "Teacher Evaluation: Informative Paragraph" (page 80) and "Online Communities in the Classroom" (page 83). *Work with a small group to evaluate the sample informative paragraph using the rubric. Which characteristics of informative writing do you notice in the paragraph?*

➤ Independent Practice

Distribute various colored pencils and "Investigate Characteristics of a Paragraph" (page 84). *As you read the paragraph on page 83, use a different color to highlight each characteristic of informative writing listed. Mark the box next to each characteristic to create a color-coded key. Now complete the sentence prompts in Part Two. Discuss your responses with a partner. Which key words or phrases helped you identify the topic sentence and the concluding sentence? How is information in the paragraph organized? How were you able to identify the characteristics of informative writing in this paragraph? What were its strengths and weaknesses? How would you strengthen the writing?*

➤ Review

Review the characteristics of informative writing as described on "Teacher Evaluation: Informative Paragraph." Discuss student responses to the sentence prompts together as a class, as time allows.

➤ Closing

You used a rubric to evaluate and analyze a sample informative paragraph with a small group. You also marked characteristics of informative writing, analyzed how you identified those qualities in the sample, and discussed your findings with a partner.

Online Communities in the Classroom

Online communities offer exciting possibilities for students and teachers. Students can use digital tools to work together in different ways. A classroom blog is still a good place to start. Blogs allow teachers to set privacy controls and reading and posting options. Another way for students to collaborate in an online environment is to create shared documents with a program such as Google Docs™. More elaborate methods of creating online classroom communities include learning management systems. Students access such programs at school or at home. For example, students might read a lesson at home, then come to class the next day prepared to discuss what they have learned. Online learning communities engage students with multiple learning styles and expand their horizons.

Teacher Notes

Grade level: appropriate
Lexile estimate: 1010L

Name(s): _____

Investigate Characteristics of a Paragraph

➤ Part One

As you read the paragraph on page 83, use a different color to highlight each characteristic of informative writing listed below. Mark the box next to each characteristic to create a color-coded key.

- ☐ Topic
- ☐ Topic sentence
- ☐ Facts and details about the topic
- ☐ Examples that explain the topic
- ☐ Transition words and phrases
- ☐ Concluding sentence

➤ Part Two

Now complete the sentence prompts. Discuss your responses with a partner.

1. I was able to identify the characteristics of informative writing in this paragraph by _____

    _____.

2. One strength in this paragraph is _____

    _____.

3. One weakness in this paragraph is _____

    _____.

4. I would strengthen this weakness by _____

    _____.

5. The key words or phrases that helped me identify the topic are _____

    _____.

6. Information in the paragraph is arranged _____

    _____.

7. I identified the organizational structure of the paragraph by _____

    _____.

8. I noticed the concluding sentence _____

    _____.

Introductory Paragraphs

➤ Objective

Students will participate in a class discussion to explore possible topics for their informative essays. They will read sample thesis statements and identify the topic of each, write their own thesis statements, and discuss with partners the information they might include in their essays. Students will brainstorm ideas and write introductory paragraphs.

➤ Introduction

You will discuss topic ideas for your informative essay with classmates. Then you will read sample thesis statements and write your own thesis statement. You will also use a graphic organizer to brainstorm ideas for your introductory paragraph. Our topic for this module is virtual reality.

➤ Instruction

In a longer informative piece such as an essay, authors may compare and contrast different aspects of the same topic. An informative essay may develop a concept or share information with readers. In an explanatory essay, the author may explain a process. The introductory paragraph for an informative essay contains a thesis statement that introduces the topic and provides a focus for the essay. In informative or explanatory writing, the thesis statement tells the main idea of the essay. This first paragraph gives readers an overview of the information that will be discussed in the body of the essay. The introductory paragraph may begin with an interesting sentence to capture readers' attention. Brainstorming and drafting an introductory paragraph will help you identify which ideas you will need to research.

➤ Guided Practice

Use an interactive whiteboard or chart paper to conduct an interactive class discussion. *Let's brainstorm possible topics about the general subject of this module: virtual reality. Which aspect of this topic interests you the most? How could you narrow this broad subject to write about a specific topic? What will you need to research to be able to write about this topic?*

Distribute "Explore a Thesis Statement" (page 86). *Read each thesis statement in Part One and underline the topic of each. What information and ideas would you expect each essay to include? Write your ideas on the lines below each thesis statement. Complete Part Two by thinking about the ideas you heard during the class discussion and the sentences you read in Part One. Use a separate piece of paper to answer the questions. Write a thesis statement for your essay. Then trade papers with a partner and read his or her thesis statement. What questions do you have about your partner's topic? What information would you expect your partner to include in his or her essay?*

➤ Independent Practice

Distribute "Map Your Concept" (page 87). *Brainstorm ideas for your introductory paragraph on the graphic organizer. How will you engage readers in your opening sentence? How did you identify and introduce your topic in your thesis statement? How will you approach your topic?* (provide information, pros and cons, compare/contrast, cause/effect, explain significance of topic, describe an object or phenomenon, problem/solution, explain a process, etc.) *What is your purpose in writing about this topic? Refer to these notes to draft an introductory paragraph for your essay.*

➤ Review

Think aloud to model brainstorming ideas for an introductory paragraph related to a specific topic to complete the graphic organizer.

➤ Closing

You chose a topic for your informative essay and wrote a thesis statement. Then you gave and received feedback. You also brainstormed a specific focus for your topic and drafted an introductory paragraph.

Explore a Thesis Statement

➤ Part One

Read each thesis statement below. Underline the topic of each. What information and ideas would you expect each essay to include? Write your ideas on the lines below each thesis statement.

1. When people wear virtual-reality headsets, they become immersed in a simulated environment that mimics the real world.

   _____

   _____

2. Healthcare professionals look to virtual-reality technology for diagnosis and treatment.

   _____

   _____

3. Virtual-reality headset applications allow scientists to control robots on Earth as well as in outer space.

   _____

   _____

4. With virtual-reality simulations, more people can experience museum collections and other cultural encounters.

   _____

   _____

5. Virtual-reality headsets may have a place in education for applications such as virtual field trips, digital simulations, and learning experiences for students with special needs.

   _____

   _____

➤ Part Two

Think about the ideas you heard during the class discussion and the sentences you read in Part One. Answer the following questions on a separate piece of paper.

1. Which idea related to this topic interests you the most?

2. What will be the topic of your informative essay?

3. Write a thesis statement for your informative essay.

Trade papers with a partner and read his or her thesis statement.

4. What questions do you have about your partner's topic?

5. What information would you expect your partner to include in his or her essay?

Map Your Concept

Brainstorm ideas for your introductory paragraph. Think about the following questions as you complete the graphic organizer below.

- How will you engage readers in your opening sentence?
- How did you identify and introduce your topic in your thesis statement?
- How will you approach your topic? (provide information, pros and cons, compare/contrast, cause/effect, explain significance of topic, describe an object or phenomenon, problem/solution, explain a process, etc.)
- What is your purpose in writing about this topic?

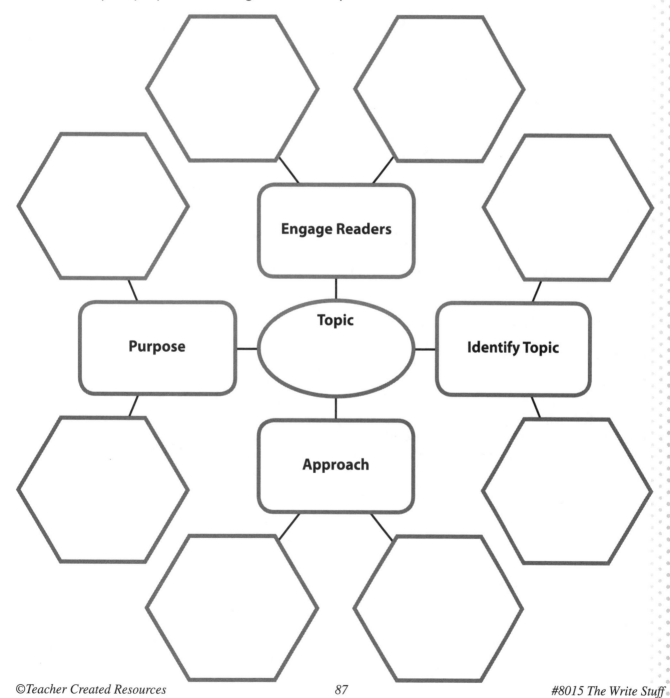

Body Paragraphs

➤ Objective

Students will research information about their topics and compile lists of sources. Then they will complete graphic organizers for their essays based on their purposes and approaches to specific topics. They will brainstorm with partners specific details to include in the body paragraphs of their essays.

➤ Introduction

You will research to learn more about your topic. Then you will complete a graphic organizer for your essay based on your specific topic and approach. You will work with a partner to brainstorm details to include in your essay.

➤ Instruction

Body paragraphs form the main part of your essay; they are the paragraphs after the introductory paragraph and before the concluding paragraph. The introductory paragraph introduces the main points, and there will be one paragraph for each main point of your essay. Each body paragraph is a complete paragraph, with a topic sentence, details about the main idea in the paragraph, and a concluding sentence.

The purpose of informative writing is to inform or explain a topic to readers. We organize information in essays in a way that makes sense. The way we organize information may depend on the specific focus of the essay. An informative essay may explain the cause and effect of something or why a certain action produces specific results. Informative writing may compare and contrast two concepts. It can also explain how to do something or how something works. Any of these essays inform readers who may not be familiar with the topic.

➤ Guided Practice

Distribute "Research Your Topic" (page 89). *Write one question about your topic using the key word captioned in each box. Use the questions you wrote to research your topic. Record what you discover in each box. List sources by number or symbol on a separate piece of paper. Then note the appropriate number or symbol for each source in each box.*

Distribute "Planning My Essay" (page 90). *Refer to your notes on "Map Your Concept" (page 87) and use what you learned in your research on "Research Your Topic" to complete the graphic organizer. Use the questions to help you.*

➤ Independent Practice

Distribute "Focus on Details" (page 91). *Concrete, specific details strengthen writing and add to readers' comprehension. Follow these tips to develop ideas in your essay: Each detail should add new and unique information to the description or explanation, information should be relevant to your topic and thesis statement, and information should explain the topic clearly to readers. Write ideas about what you could include in your essay for each type of detail in the graphic organizer. Discuss with a partner what you have learned about your topic from your research. Ask your partner to contribute his or her ideas for specific details to add to your notes.*

Then use your notes and ideas from the activities in this lesson to write body paragraphs for your essay.

➤ Review

Provide resources for student research and demonstrate how to create a key for a list of sources. Review the preferred format for bibliographic information.

➤ Closing

You researched information related to your topic and took notes. Then you created an outline for your essay and brainstormed ideas for specific details to include in your body paragraphs.

Name(s): _____

Research Your Topic

- Write one question about your topic using the key word captioned in each box.
- Use the questions to research your topic. Record what you discover in each box.
- List sources by number or symbol on a separate piece of paper. Then note the appropriate number or symbol for each source in each box.

What?	**When?**

Who?	**Where?**

Why?	**How?**

Name(s): _____

Planning My Essay

Refer to your notes on "Map Your Concept" (page 87) and use what you learned in your research on "Research Your Topic" (page 89) to complete the graphic organizer below. Use the following questions to help you:

- How can you connect your main ideas to make sense for readers?
- How will you organize the information in your essay?
- How will your organizational structure reflect your purpose?
- Which nonfiction text features would add to readers' comprehension of your information?

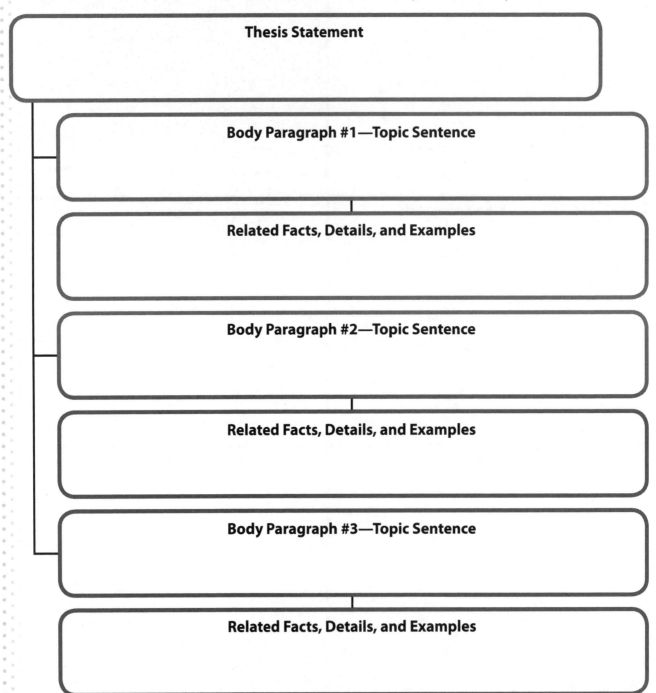

Thesis Statement

Body Paragraph #1—Topic Sentence

Related Facts, Details, and Examples

Body Paragraph #2—Topic Sentence

Related Facts, Details, and Examples

Body Paragraph #3—Topic Sentence

Related Facts, Details, and Examples

Name(s): _____

Focus on Details

Concrete, specific details strengthen the writing and add to readers' comprehension. Follow these tips to develop ideas in your essay:

- Each detail should add new and unique information to the description or explanation.
- Information should be relevant to your topic and thesis statement.
- Information should explain the topic clearly to readers.

Write ideas about what you could include in your essay for each type of detail in the graphic organizer below.

Discuss with a partner what you have learned about your topic from your research. Ask your partner to contribute his or her ideas for specific details to add to your notes.

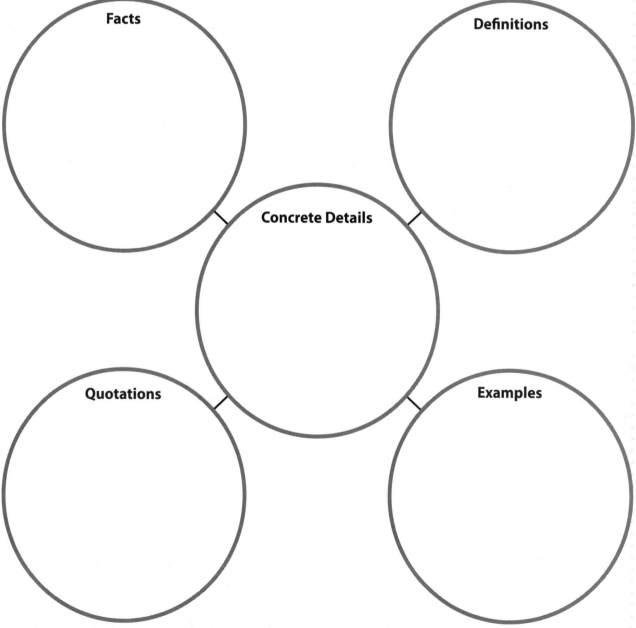

Concluding Paragraphs

➤ Objective

Students will read a sample informative essay and write anonymous sample concluding paragraphs. They will discuss the effectiveness of their paragraphs in small groups. Then they will share ideas for different approaches for a concluding paragraph with partners and write concluding paragraphs for their own essays.

➤ Introduction

You will read an informative paragraph and write a sample concluding paragraph for it. You will discuss with a small group the characteristics of an effective concluding paragraph and evaluate your sample paragraphs as examples. Then you will share ideas with a partner for different ways to approach a concluding paragraph and write a concluding paragraph for your own essay.

➤ Instruction

The concluding paragraph in an informative essay summarizes the main points. It restates the main idea or thesis statement of the essay with a deeper understanding of the topic. A concluding sentence in the paragraph emphasizes the importance of the topic. The concluding paragraph in an explanatory essay will include the final step in the process. It may provide an overview of what has just been explained in the essay.

➤ Guided Practice

Distribute "An Effective Concluding Paragraph" (page 93). *Read the essay and write a concluding paragraph, without writing your name on your work. If possible, have students use technology to make their writing anonymous. Work in small groups to discuss your sample concluding paragraphs. Place the paragraphs in a pile and shuffle them to keep each person's work anonymous. What characteristics does an effective concluding paragraph have? Read each paragraph and discuss how well it summarizes the essay. In what ways do the paragraphs effectively conclude the essay?*

➤ Independent Practice

Distribute "Write a Concluding Paragraph" (page 94). *Review your thesis statement and how your essay presents concepts and information. Discuss the list of possible approaches for a concluding paragraph with a partner. Which idea might work well for an effective concluding paragraph for your essay? Write a concluding paragraph for your informative essay in the space provided.*

➤ Review

Display samples of informative essays from classroom resources to review the characteristics of effective concluding paragraphs. Go over the different approaches to writing a concluding paragraph to answer questions and clarify as needed.

➤ Closing

You wrote a sample concluding paragraph for an informative essay and discussed your writing with a small group. Then you reviewed various approaches with a partner and wrote a concluding paragraph for your own informative essay.

Name(s): _____

An Effective Concluding Paragraph

More than one virtual-reality company has plans to bring this new technology to public-school classrooms. Developers believe it will engage students in a variety of ways. The headsets could be used for virtual field trips, digital simulations, and learning experiences for students with special needs.

With virtual reality, students can explore places beyond the reach of their local communities. Virtual reality brings museums and other physical locations related to topics of study to the classroom. Consumers have had access to the concept for over fifty years. Handheld stereoscopes were sold with cardboard reels that contained pairs of small 3-D color photographs. Virtual-reality headsets take the experience an important step further. Now viewers experience sound and movement in addition to images.

The addition of sound and movement makes digital simulations possible. Students can observe and participate in activities such as mathematics explorations and science experiments. This expands the horizons of what students can experience. They apply concepts they are learning in practical ways.

Another practical application of VR headsets is using the devices with students who have special needs. The technology is capable of being programmed to offset students' limitations. This would enable them to complete tasks they might not otherwise be able to perform. Virtual reality engages users and provides sensory input, which can be beneficial to some children. Students develop hand-eye coordination and other physical and cognitive skills by interacting with gaming consoles. Some technology is available for teachers and students in schools with limited resources.

> ## Teacher Notes
>
> Grade level: appropriate
> Lexile estimate: 1010L

Name(s): _____

Write a Concluding Paragraph

Review your thesis statement and how your essay presents concepts and information. Discuss the list of possible approaches for a concluding paragraph with a partner. Which idea(s) might work well for an effective concluding paragraph for your essay?

- Restating the main idea
- Summarizing main points
- Reviewing the effect in a cause-and-effect essay
- Emphasizing the result of an action
- Explaining the significance of the topic for readers
- Leaving a reflective thought with readers
- Suggesting an action readers might take based on the information presented
- Offering your unique perspective on the thesis statement
- Making a prediction

Write a concluding paragraph for your informative essay on the lines below.

_____

_____

_____

_____

_____

_____

_____

_____

_____

_____

_____

_____

_____

_____

_____

_____

_____

_____

First Draft and Peer Review

➤ Objective

Students will write first drafts of their informative essays. Then they will review the characteristics of informative writing, read classmates' essays, and ask questions about their partners' writing. They will also offer constructive feedback on their partners' essays.

➤ Introduction

You will use your notes from previous activities in this module to write a first draft of your informative essay. You will also review the characteristics of effective informative writing. Then you will read a partner's essay and write questions you have about his or her writing. You will also complete sentence prompts to give constructive feedback to your partner.

➤ Instruction

When you write the first draft of your informative essay, incorporate all your notes from brainstorming and research. Start with the sentence to capture your readers' attention and your thesis statement from "Explore a Thesis Statement" (page 86) and "Map Your Concept" (page 87) to write an introductory paragraph. Be sure to introduce the main points you will discuss in your essay. Use your notes and outline from "Research Your Topic" (page 89), "Planning My Essay" (page 90), and "Focus on Details" (page 91) to review the body paragraphs you have written. Add the concluding paragraph you wrote on "Write a Concluding Paragraph" (page 94).

➤ Guided Practice

Distribute "Strengthen Your Writing" (page 96). *When peers review our writing, we receive ideas for how to make our writing better. This is the first step in the revision process. As you read your partner's essay, keep the characteristics of effective informative writing listed in Part One in mind. How has your partner's use of concise, descriptive words helped you understand the topic? How is the essay organized? How well did the author use transition words and phrases to connect ideas, sentences, and paragraphs within the essay? After you read your partner's essay, write two or three questions you have about the writing. Then ask your partner the questions and record his or her answers.*

➤ Independent Practice

Use your thoughts about the writing as well as your partner's responses to complete several of the sentence prompts in Part Two to offer constructive feedback to your partner. How will the feedback you received help you revise your essay?

➤ Review

Go over what it means to offer constructive feedback: the goal is to help classmates make their essays better and to strengthen their writing based on the characteristics of effective informative writing.

➤ Closing

You wrote a first draft of your informative essay and reviewed the characteristics of effective informative writing. Then you read a classmate's essay and asked and answered questions about your writing. You also gave your partner constructive feedback about his or her essay.

Name(s): _____

Strengthen Your Writing

➤ Part One

1. Read the following characteristics of effective informative writing:

Introductory Paragraph	My essay has an introductory paragraph that introduces a topic about virtual reality clearly and in an interesting way. It has a clear thesis statement.
Organization	Related information and ideas in my essay are organized in a logical way to emphasize specific points about virtual reality.
Details	My essay has facts, definitions, concrete details, and examples that clearly develop my topic about virtual reality.
Transition Words	I use a variety of transition words to connect ideas about the main point of each paragraph in my essay.
Concluding Paragraph	My essay has a concluding paragraph that summarizes the information and restates the main idea about virtual reality.

2. Read your partner's informative essay.

3. Write two or three questions you have about your partner's essay. Leave space for responses. Refer to the characteristics of informative writing listed above for ideas.

    _____

    _____

    _____

    _____

    _____

    _____

4. Ask your partner the questions you have written and record his or her responses on the lines above.

➤ Part Two

Complete the writing prompts to give your partner feedback on his or her informative essay. Use a separate piece of paper.

- My favorite part was _____ because . . .
- One thing I learned from reading your essay is . . .
- One way to make this stronger could be . . .
- Did you ever think about . . .
- I am not sure who your audience is because . . .

Second Draft and Self-Evaluation

➤ Objective

Students will review the self-evaluation rubric and make revision notes on their first drafts. They will use their notes and feedback from classmates to write second drafts of their informative essays. Then they will use the rubric to evaluate their second drafts and consider reflection questions.

➤ Introduction

You will preview a rubric of qualities of informative writing. Then you will use the revision notes and peer feedback on your first draft to write a second draft of your informative essay. You will use the rubric to evaluate your second draft and answer reflection questions to revise your writing for a final draft.

➤ Instruction

The rubric we are using today is similar to the one you used to evaluate your informative paragraph. What have you learned since then about informative writing? Discuss with students. *As you use the rubric to evaluate your writing, think about the strengths and weaknesses you notice in your essay. In which areas did you give yourself higher or lower scores? When you think about changes you want to make in your second draft, you make decisions about improving your writing.*

➤ Guided Practice

Let's review the specific characteristics of an informative essay that I will look for when I read your essays. Distribute "Self-Evaluation: Informative Essay" (page 98). *Read through the first draft of your essay. Note any revisions you want to make based on our discussion of the rubric. Use the feedback you received from a classmate on "Strengthen Your Writing" (page 96) and make additional comments about changes you will make to your first draft. Write a second draft of your informative essay.*

➤ Independent Practice

After you have written your second draft, use the "Self-Evaluation: Informative Essay" rubric to evaluate and score your writing. How does the rubric help you form an opinion about the effectiveness of your writing? What strengths and weaknesses do you notice in your essay? What could you add to better inform readers about the topic? What could you change to more clearly present your information to help readers understand the subject? How well does your essay reflect a purpose and convey the importance of the topic for readers? Write your responses and revision notes on your second draft.

➤ Review

Answer any questions students have about the rubric. As time allows, discuss examples and revisions that could be made to a draft in response to the reflection questions in Independent Practice. Encourage students to use technology resources to produce their final drafts.

➤ Closing

You previewed a rubric and made notes on your first draft about things you wanted to revise. Then you wrote a second draft of your essay and used the rubric to evaluate your writing. Use the self-evaluation rubric, your responses to the reflection questions, and revision notes to write a final draft of your informative essay and bring it back to class for the next lesson.

Self-Evaluation: Informative Essay

Name: _____   Score: _____

	4	3	2	1
Introductory Paragraph	My essay has an introductory paragraph that introduces a topic about virtual reality clearly and in an interesting way. It has a clear thesis statement.	My essay has an introductory paragraph with a clear thesis statement about virtual reality.	My essay has an introductory paragraph that mentions the topic of virtual reality.	The topic of my essay is unclear in the introductory paragraph.
Organization	Related information and ideas in my essay are organized in a logical way to emphasize specific points about virtual reality.	Related information and ideas about virtual reality are grouped together in paragraphs.	Some information and ideas about virtual reality are grouped together.	Information and ideas about virtual reality are not organized in a way that makes sense.
Details	My essay has facts, definitions, concrete details, and examples that clearly develop my topic about virtual reality.	My essay has facts, definitions, details, and examples about virtual reality.	My essay has some details, such as facts, definitions, or examples, about virtual reality.	My essay does not have many details about virtual reality.
Transition Words	I use a variety of transition words to connect ideas about the main point of each paragraph in my essay.	I use transition words to connect ideas within each paragraph of my essay.	I use at least one transition word to connect ideas within my essay.	My essay does not have any transition words to connect ideas.
Concluding Paragraph	My essay has a concluding paragraph that summarizes the information and restates the main idea about virtual reality.	My essay has a concluding paragraph that closely relates to my main point about virtual reality.	My essay has a concluding paragraph about virtual reality.	My essay does not have a clear concluding paragraph, or the concluding paragraph is not about virtual reality.
Conventions	Sentences are complete, and there are very few errors in grammar, word usage, capitalization, punctuation, and spelling.	Most of the sentences are complete. Any errors in grammar, word usage, capitalization, punctuation, or spelling do not affect the meaning of the writing.	Some of the sentences are incomplete. There are errors in grammar, word usage, capitalization, punctuation, or spelling that make the writing hard to read and understand.	Many of the sentences are incomplete. There are many errors in grammar, word usage, capitalization, punctuation, or spelling that make the writing hard to read and understand.

Review

➤ Objective

Students will read a sample informative essay and comment on how well it meets the characteristics of informative writing. Then they will share their comments with classmates and ask and answer questions about the essay. They will also write recommendations based on their evaluation of the writing.

➤ Introduction

You will read a sample informative essay and critique the writing for how well it meets qualities of effective informative writing. You will share your comments with classmates and ask and answer questions about the essay. Then you will write a recommendation of the essay based on your critique.

➤ Instruction

What are the characteristics of informative and explanatory essays? Discuss with the class. *The focused review you did of a classmate's draft and the rubric you completed to evaluate your own writing summarized key features of this type of writing. As you read a sample essay today, consider how the author communicated ideas and information in a way that added to readers' understanding of the topic.*

➤ Guided Practice

Distribute "Virtual-Reality Headsets" (page 100), "Critique an Informative Essay" (page 101), and "Self-Evaluation: Informative Essay" (page 98). *Read the sample essay on page 100 and then complete Part One of the activity on page 101. Read through the essay again, focusing on the introductory paragraph. Write a comment about how well that paragraph meets the qualities of this characteristic as described on "Self-Evaluation: Informative Essay." What are the strengths or weaknesses of the essay in this area?*

Turn to a classmate and share your comment for the introductory paragraph. Repeat steps 2–4, focusing on the organization of the essay. Continue for the details, transition words, and concluding paragraph of the essay.

➤ Independent Practice

Complete Part Two of "Critique an Informative Essay." Write one or two questions for a classmate to answer about the effectiveness of the essay. Trade papers and answer a classmate's questions about the essay. Then write a recommendation for the essay explaining why you would or would not recommend others read the essay.

➤ Review

Review the concept of writing critiques: analyzing writing objectively for strengths as well as weaknesses and how well the author accomplished his or her purpose. Discuss what it means to write a recommendation of a piece for others to read.

➤ Closing

You read an informative essay and critiqued its strengths and weaknesses based on how well it meets characteristics of effective informative writing. Then you discussed your comments with classmates and wrote a recommendation of the piece for others.

Name(s): _____

Virtual-Reality Headsets

When people wear virtual-reality headsets, they become immersed in a simulated environment that mimics the real world. A VR headset covers a person's eyes and sometimes ears so that they actually wear a screen. Users experience the sights and sounds of the virtual world. Although people associate these headsets primarily with gaming, they have other uses too.

Game designers take players anywhere, from the dawn of the dinosaurs to World War II. Users might experience kart-racing or a roller-coaster ride. Virtual reality allows players to see and hear the experience as if they were actually there.

Some companies have also designed VR headsets for the classroom. Students wear a headset to view and experience a virtual world. Teachers can create virtual tours and objects for their students. This expands the experiences and materials teachers can incorporate into learning experiences. Imagine being able to learn about the inner workings of a computer. Virtual field trips might include destinations such as outer space, the zoo, or deep-sea adventures.

Outside the classroom, people use virtual-reality headsets for other forms of education as well. The military uses the devices for training before soldiers enter the field. Driver-training programs use simulated environments to educate people about the dangers of distracted driving.

Virtual headsets have changed the way people view and interact with the world—forever. Several different types of VR headsets are on the market with a wide range of programs. Many of these virtual-reality applications will benefit people in the real world.

Teacher Notes

Grade level: appropriate

Lexile estimate: 970L

Name(s): _____

Critique an Informative Essay

➤ Part One

1. Read the sample essay "Virtual-Reality Headsets" (page 100).

2. Read through the essay again, focusing on the introductory paragraph.

3. In the corresponding row below, write a comment about how well that paragraph meets the qualities of this characteristic as described on "Self-Evaluation: Informative Essay" (page 98).

4. Turn to a classmate and share your comment for the introductory paragraph.

5. Repeat steps 2–4, focusing on the organization of the essay.

6. Continue for the details, transition words, and concluding paragraph of the essay.

Characteristic	Comments
Introductory Paragraph	
Organization	
Details	
Transition Words	
Concluding Paragraph	

➤ Part Two

1. Write one or two questions for a classmate to answer about the effectiveness of the essay.

    _____

    _____

    _____

2. Trade papers and answer a classmate's questions about the essay on a separate piece of paper.

3. Then write a recommendation explaining why you would or would not recommend others read the essay.

Final Evaluation

➤ Objective

Students will compare the scores they gave their writing on a self-evaluation with scores they received from the teacher using a similar rubric. Then they will work in small groups to average scores anonymously and make observations about the differences between individual and averaged scores and student and teacher scores. They will also answer and discuss response questions.

➤ Introduction

You will compare the scores you gave your writing on a self-evaluation with the scores you received from me based on a similar rubric. Then you will work with a small group to average your scores to create a composite chart. You will answer and discuss questions about your observations of the data.

➤ Instruction

You evaluated your informative essay using the "Self-Evaluation: Informative Essay" (page 98) rubric. This showed you the characteristics I would look for when I scored your essays. When you used the rubric, you also wrote responses to reflection questions to revise your second draft. When you compare your scores with those you received from me, you will also create an anonymous group composite score chart to compare your scores within a group.

➤ Guided Practice

Distribute "An Overview of My Writing" (page 104) and students' copies of "Self-Evaluation: Informative Essay" and "Teacher Evaluation: Informative Essay" (page 103). *Record your scores from each of the evaluation sheets on the chart. Work with a small group to average your scores to create a group composite chart of scores. Review the composite chart with members of the group.*

➤ Independent Practice

Answer the questions about your observations on a separate piece of paper. Then share your responses with classmates in your small group.

➤ Review

Review how to average a set of numbers and what we can observe from such calculations (provides an overview of students' writing progress, a view of the class progress as a whole, a discussion point for small groups of students).

➤ Closing

You recorded your scores from a self-evaluation and a teacher evaluation to compare the differences. Then you created a chart of group scores and discussed the average scores, similarities and differences, and what we learned from such data.

Teacher Evaluation: Informative Essay

Student Name: _____ **Score:** _____

	4	3	2	1
Introductory Paragraph	The essay has an introductory paragraph that introduces a topic about virtual reality clearly and in an interesting way. It has a clear thesis statement.	The essay has an introductory paragraph with a clear thesis statement about virtual reality.	The essay has an introductory paragraph that mentions the topic of virtual reality.	The topic of the essay is unclear in the introductory paragraph.
Organization	Related information and ideas in the essay are organized in a logical way to emphasize specific points about virtual reality.	Related information and ideas about virtual reality are grouped together in paragraphs.	Some information and ideas about virtual reality are grouped together.	Information and ideas about virtual reality are not organized in a way that makes sense.
Details	The essay has facts, definitions, concrete details, and examples that clearly develop the topic about virtual reality.	The essay has facts, definitions, details, and examples about virtual reality.	The essay has some details, such as facts, definitions, or examples, about virtual reality.	The essay does not have many details about virtual reality.
Transition Words	The author uses a variety of transition words to connect ideas about the main point of each paragraph in the essay.	The author uses transition words to connect ideas within each paragraph of the essay.	The author uses at least one transition word to connect ideas within the essay.	The essay does not have any transition words to connect ideas.
Concluding Paragraph	The essay has a concluding paragraph that summarizes the information and restates the main idea about virtual reality.	The essay has a concluding paragraph that closely relates to the main point about virtual reality.	The essay has a concluding paragraph about virtual reality.	The essay does not have a clear concluding paragraph, or the concluding paragraph is not about virtual reality.
Conventions	Sentences are complete, and there are very few errors in grammar, word usage, capitalization, punctuation, and spelling.	Most of the sentences are complete. Any errors in grammar, word usage, capitalization, punctuation, or spelling do not affect the meaning of the writing.	Some of the sentences are incomplete. There are errors in grammar, word usage, capitalization, punctuation, or spelling that make the writing hard to read and understand.	Many of the sentences are incomplete. There are many errors in grammar, word usage, capitalization, punctuation, or spelling that make the writing hard to read and understand.

Name(s): _____

An Overview of My Writing

1. Record your scores from "Self-Evaluation: Informative Essay" (page 98) and "Teacher Evaluation: Informative Essay" (page 103) on the chart at the bottom of the page.

2. Work with a small group to average your scores to create a group composite chart of scores.

3. Review the composite chart.

4. Answer the following response questions on a separate piece of paper. Discuss your answers within your small group.

   - Where do each of your scores fall compared to others in the group?
   - How do you think student and teacher perspectives on writing differ?
   - What differences between student and teacher scores do you notice?
   - Why do you think these differences exist?
   - What do we learn from these averaged scores?
   - How can you use what you learned from this activity to improve your writing?

Self-Evaluation Scores	Characteristic	Teacher Evaluation Scores
	Introductory Paragraph	
	Organization	
	Details	
	Transition Words	
	Concluding Paragraph	
	Conventions	

All About Narrative Writing

➤ Objective

Students will read and discuss sample narrative paragraphs to create a class-generated chart of characteristics of narrative writing. Then they will work with partners to observe narrative characteristics in additional paragraphs and create their own charts to list those characteristics.

➤ Introduction

You will read and observe characteristics of narrative writing demonstrated in sample paragraphs. You will create a chart of narrative writing characteristics to guide you as you write your own narrative paragraphs. Our topic for this module is volunteer experiences.

➤ Instruction

Narrative writing describes a real or imagined experience by using descriptive details to relate a sequence of actions within an event and show the responses of people to a situation. The experience happens to one or more individuals, also known as characters. Narratives often describe a personal experience that happened to the narrator. A narrative begins by introducing the narrator or main character, setting, and situation. The conclusion flows naturally from the narrated experience or event. Readers may learn a lesson or gain insight from reading the account.

➤ Guided Practice

Display and photocopy "Orphanage Adventure" (page 106) and "Classroom Buddies" (page 107), covering up the Teacher Notes. Distribute the narratives. *What do you notice about these examples of narrative paragraphs? What characteristics does each paragraph have?* Create a T-chart with one column titled "Orphanage Adventure" and the other column titled "Classroom Buddies." *Let's create a chart to list the characteristics of effective narrative writing we notice in each sample paragraph. What makes narrative writing engaging and relevant for readers? Which paragraph is stronger? Why do you think this?*

➤ Independent Practice

Distribute "Community Service" (page 109, strong example), "Neighbors Helping Neighbors" (page 110, weak example), and "What We Notice About Narrative Writing" (page 108). *What do you notice about the characteristics of narrative writing in each sample paragraph? Work with a partner to identify and describe on the chart narrative characteristics in each paragraph. How will this observation activity help you as you learn about and practice writing a narrative paragraph?*

➤ Review

Refer to the qualities of narrative writing as presented during the lesson to review and go over students' responses on "What We Notice About Narrative Writing."

➤ Closing

You read sample paragraphs and identified the characteristics of narrative writing demonstrated in each. You worked with classmates to create a What We Notice chart to guide you as you write your own narrative paragraphs.

Name(s): _____

Orphanage Adventure

As we pulled up to the orphanage, my excitement mounted. My first time in a different country, I was here on a volunteer work trip with my family as part of a larger group. We would perform maintenance at the orphanage and help out taking care of the kids while the caregivers had the opportunity to do errands. I'd been warned that it would be hot and we would work hard, but I knew our work would be important. When we got our assignments, I was placed with the outdoor crew since I was more adventurous than some of the other kids who had come along with their families. At first, I was disappointed, but once I joined the work crew, I made my two best friends for the summer. We weeded the vegetable garden, dug water irrigation trenches, raked leaves, and trimmed the palm trees. As we had been warned, it got unbelievably hot, but that didn't bother us. We traded jokes and came up with catchphrases for the trip. I did get my chance to work with the girls who lived in the orphanage when one of the volunteers fell ill. I had a morning and afternoon with them, so I helped get them up and ready for the day. Once they had rubbed the sleep out of their eyes, I could tell these girls were special. We played games with them and listened to them tell stories about their families. Even though these girls had so little, they had such big hearts. When I visited their orphanage, my goal was to benefit them, but they helped me understand that life is so much more than what we see. It's about loving with everything you have, and when you think you have nothing else to give, give even more.

Teacher Notes

This narrative paragraph has the following strengths and weaknesses:

- The beginning sentence introduces a narrator and a setting, but the situation is introduced in a different sentence.
- Actions within the experience are narrated in a logical order that makes sense.
- Sensory details and concrete words describe the actions that happen in the experience.
- Descriptions and actions show how the narrator reacted to what happened in the experience.
- Transition words guide readers through the narrative.
- The author writes with a sense of audience and makes the narrative relevant for readers.
- The concluding sentence provides a sense of closure with the author's reflection of the experience.

> Grade level: appropriate
> Lexile estimate: 1020L

Classroom Buddies

I eagerly anticipated my opportunity to volunteer at the day-care center next door to our school. As part of a "buddy" program, my class would visit with the preschool children who attended the center. As we walked down the hall to the preschool room, toddler cries and whimpers mingled with children's chatter. I wondered what we had in store for us. Our teacher introduced us to Wanda, the preschool teacher. A small boy gripped Wanda's hand and sucked the thumb of his other hand. Wanda gave us a tour of the classroom, including where to find paper towels and tissues, activities we could do with the children, and most importantly, where the animal crackers were kept. I could only imagine the significance of those. A toddler arrived and, as her parent left to go to work, she began to cry, although I would describe it as more of a howl. Wanda was busy with another child, so I tried to distract the little girl with a musical toy, then a soft puppy stuffed animal, but nothing seemed to work. "Give her an animal cracker,"

Wanda said. I rushed to the giant jar and pulled it down. As soon as the toddler heard the scraping of the lid being twisted off, her wailing subsided. "Want a cookie?" I asked her, and she sniffed and nodded. Though that wasn't my only trial on my first day at the day-care center, it was my most memorable, because I was able to console a crying child. After that, the little girl became one of my biggest fans.

Teacher Notes

This narrative paragraph has the following strengths and weaknesses.

- The beginning sentence introduces a narrator, setting, and situation.
- Actions within the narrative experience are described in chronological order.
- Only some of the descriptions and actions show how the character responds to things that happen in the narrative.
- Transition words and phrases guide readers through the things that happen as part of the narrative experience.
- The concluding sentence flows naturally after the described experience.

> Grade level: appropriate
> Lexile estimate: 940L

Name(s): _____

What We Notice About Narrative Writing

1. Read "Community Service" (page 109).

2. What do you notice about the characteristics of narrative writing demonstrated in this paragraph? Describe each aspect of the narrative on the chart below.

3. Read "Neighbors Helping Neighbors" (page 110).

4. What do you notice about the characteristics of narrative writing demonstrated in this paragraph? Describe each aspect of the narrative on the chart below.

5. Which paragraph is more effective? Why?

    _____

    _____

    _____

Characteristic	Community Service	Neighbors Helping Neighbors
Beginning Sentence		
Organization		
Descriptions		
Actions		
Transition Words		
Concluding Sentence		

6. How will this observation activity help you as you learn about and practice writing a narrative paragraph?

    _____

    _____

    _____

Name(s): _____

Community Service

Last week, my friends and I planned a gathering to work together on our community service project. Students at our school are required to do one project per term. We are allowed to choose what we want to do, as long as we have the teacher's approval. My friends had several ideas, but finally we decided to write letters to veterans and people still serving in the military. Our school has access to a program that delivers the letters. It also provides guidelines for us for our protection as well as those receiving the letters. One of my friends has an uncle serving in the military. She suggested we pretend we were writing to someone we knew, although we would have to follow the guidelines for topics of conversation. At first, I had trouble getting started, but then it got easier as I remembered to think of the other person. Reading a letter lets us know someone else is thinking of us, and that's one of the greatest services we can do for other people!

> ### Teacher Notes
> Grade level: appropriate
> Lexile estimate: 970L

Name(s): _____

Neighbors Helping Neighbors

Dad carried the ladder and his toolbox, and I held some twist ties and a decoration as we walked next door to Mrs. Simons' house. Our elderly neighbor loved to decorate for the holidays, but her husband had died during the year, and now she had no one to help her. I greeted our friend and handed her the decoration I had made. Then I followed Dad outside to unwind strings of lights and hand them up to him while he stood on the ladder. A slight breeze blew and clouds blocked the sun, but it didn't look like it would rain. I shoved the twist ties into my pocket so they would be handy if needed. Then I carefully lifted the first strand of lights out and set it on the grass. Fortunately, Mr. Simons had neatly wound them the year before when he put them away. With the hooks he had put on the eaves still in place, Dad's job was easy, too. In no time at all, we had strings of white lights strung across the eaves of the house and up the walkway. Mrs. Simons came outside to admire our handiwork and declared it looked very festive. Then she invited us in for hot apple cider and banana bread, which sounded good to me!

Teacher Notes

Grade level: below
Lexile estimate: 730L

Beginning the Narrative

➤ Objective
Students will use a thesaurus and other resources to brainstorm descriptive words to introduce narrators or characters, settings, and contexts for their narrated experiences. They will complete graphic organizers as they work with partners. Then they will list specific actions that happened as part of the experiences.

➤ Introduction
You will work with a partner to brainstorm descriptive words to introduce a narrator or character and setting for your narrative experience. You will also complete a graphic organizer to list the actions that happened as part of the experience.

➤ Instruction
Within the first sentence of a short narrative piece, authors orient their readers. This means they introduce one or more main characters in a setting, and introduce a story event through the point of view of the person telling the story. Before writing the entire narrative, you will want to plan and organize the sequence of actions within the experience of your story. Narratives include details in an order that makes sense. The details help readers understand the author's purpose in telling the story.

➤ Guided Practice
Distribute "Introduce a Character" (page 112). *Think about the narrator or main character in your narrative and where the experience takes place. What words can you use to introduce the narrator and/or main character(s)? How will your description paint a mental picture for readers? Discuss your ideas with a partner and use a thesaurus to brainstorm descriptive words for your character. Write the words in the box. Then write one or two sentences to introduce the character within the context of the narrative experience. This will not be your final beginning sentence, but a draft of your ideas so far.*

Distribute "Orient Readers" (page 113). *Within the first one or two sentences, authors also introduce the setting and situation. Gather information about the experience you will describe in your narrative. For example, view personal or online pictures of people engaged in a volunteer experience, review any notes you have about a volunteer experience, talk with people who participated in an experience similar to the one you will be describing, or review images from the location the experience took place or could take place. Write concrete words and actions to describe your impressions of the setting and context of the situation in the boxes. Then review your notes on "Introduce a Character." Work with a partner to write a sentence that introduces a narrator or character and setting and establishes the context of the narrative situation.*

➤ Independent Practice
Distribute "Actions Within the Experience" (page 114). *Brainstorm actions that happened within the experience. Write one or more words in the center circle to identify the narrative experience. Then write one action of a character in each circle. Show the actions using specific verbs and nouns. Think about the actions as if you are experiencing what happened right now. Include specific sensory details to describe the actions.*

➤ Review
Review the difference between "showing" and "telling" and how to maintain a consistent point of view within a narrative. Discuss the importance of relating actions with the experience in a logical order.

➤ Closing
You worked with a partner to brainstorm descriptive words to introduce your narrator or main character. You also completed graphic organizers to orient readers to the setting and situation, as well as planning the actions that take place within the experience.

Introduce a Character

Think about the narrator or main character in your narrative and where the experience takes place. Read the questions below and take notes to brainstorm details about your narrator and/or main character(s).

1. Who is the narrator or main character in your narrative?

   _____

2. What will that person be doing in the narrative?

   _____

   _____

3. What words can you use to introduce the narrator and/or main character(s)?

   _____

   _____

   _____

4. How will your description paint a mental picture for readers?

   _____

   _____

   _____

5. Discuss your ideas with a partner and use a thesaurus to brainstorm descriptive words for your character. Write the words in the box below.

   ┌───┐
   │   │
   │   │
   │   │
   │   │
   └───┘

6. Write one or two sentences to introduce the character within the context of the narrative experience.

   _____

   _____

   _____

   _____

Name(s): _____

Orient Readers

Within the first one or two sentences, authors also introduce the setting and situation. Gather information about the experience you will describe in your narrative.

- View personal or online pictures of people engaged in a volunteer experience.
- Review any notes you have about a volunteer experience.
- If possible, talk with people who participated in an experience similar to the one you will be describing.
- Review images from the location where the experience took place or could take place.

Write concrete words and actions to describe your impressions of the setting and context of the situation in the boxes below.

Location	My Experience Notes

Participants

Review your notes on "Introduce a Character" (page 112). Work with a partner to write a sentence that introduces a narrator or character and setting and establishes the context of the narrative situation.

_____

_____

_____

Name(s): _____

Actions Within the Experience

Brainstorm actions that happened within the experience. Consider these tips as you complete the graphic organizer below.

- Write one or more words in the center circle to identify the narrative experience.
- Write one action of a character in each circle.
- Show the actions using specific verbs and nouns.
- Think about the actions as if you are experiencing what happened right now.
- Include specific sensory details to describe the actions.

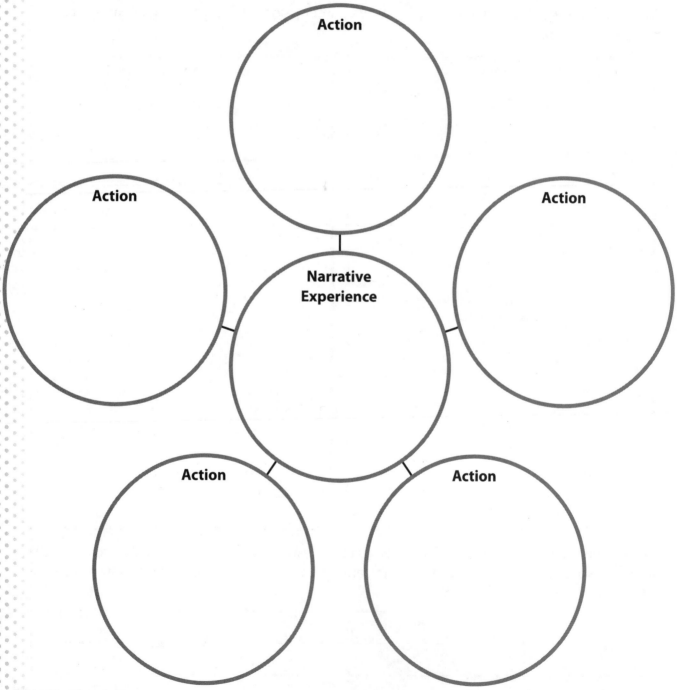

Describing the Experience

➤ Objective

Students will interview classmates about narrative experiences to acquire descriptive words and language to enrich their thinking as they write sentences for their own paragraphs. Then they will share their sentences with partners and receive feedback about perceived connotations of words they included in their writing.

➤ Introduction

Today you will interview classmates to gather ideas of descriptive words and write sentences for your narrative paragraph. Then you will share your sentences with a partner to discuss word connotations in your writing.

➤ Instruction

Authors use concrete words and sensory details to describe events and experiences in narratives. They describe how characters respond to situations in the stories. Descriptive details provide readers with mental pictures about what happens in the narrative. One way to do this is to use figurative language such as similes or metaphors. Concrete word choice helps readers understand actions within a story event.

➤ Guided Practice

Distribute "Helping Hands" (page 116). *Write questions to ask classmates about volunteer experiences. On the hand outlines, write descriptive words and phrases you hear from your classmates. Listen for concrete words that exactly describe people, places, objects, and things that happen during the experience; descriptive details that are relevant to the experience; sensory language that describes what characters see, hear, touch, smell, or taste during the experience; and how the narrator and other characters react to things that happen within the experience. As time allows, work with a classmate to investigate additional words using a thesaurus. Add words related to your narrative in the hands. Use your notes from "Introduce a Character" (page 112), "Orient Readers" (page 113), "Actions Within the Experience" (page 114), and the descriptive words you heard from classmates to write the body of your narrative paragraph on a separate piece of paper.*

➤ Independent Practice

Distribute "Word Connotations" (page 117) and highlighters. *Connotation has to do with the emotions we attach to the meaning of a word and the way it is used. Another way to think of this is to consider the ideas, mental pictures, or feelings we associate with particular words. Choose words carefully to make sure your readers understand exactly what you intend to say. When describing narrative experiences related to our topic for this unit, focus on positive connotations to engage readers. Share the sentences you wrote on "Helping Hands" with a partner. Highlight words that stand out to you in your partner's sentences. Then write each word you highlighted on the top line of a separate box. What other words, ideas, mental pictures, or emotions do you associate with each word? Write your thoughts about each word on the lines in its box.*

➤ Review

Review examples of words with positive or negative connotations from classroom resources and discuss how word choice affects readers' understanding. Model how to choose relevant and effective words for a narrative experience as needed.

➤ Closing

You talked with classmates to brainstorm descriptive words related to your narrative experience and then wrote sentences for your paragraph. Then you shared your writing with a partner to receive feedback on word connotations in your writing.

Helping Hands

Write questions to ask classmates about volunteer experiences.

① _____

② _____

③ _____

④ _____

On the hand outlines, write descriptive words and phrases you hear from your classmates. Listen for the following:

- concrete words that exactly describe people, places, objects, and things that happen during the experience
- descriptive details that are relevant to the experience
- sensory language that describes what characters see, hear, touch, smell, or taste during the experience
- how the narrator and other characters react to things that happen within the experience

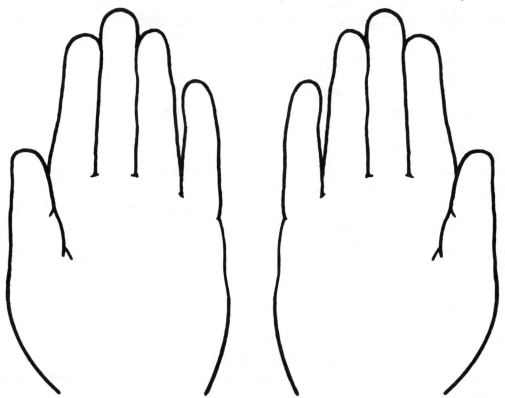

As time allows, work with a classmate to investigate additional words using a thesaurus. Add words related to your narrative in the hands above.

Use your notes from "Introduce a Character" (page 112), "Orient Readers" (page 113), "Actions Within the Experience" (page 114), and the descriptive words you heard from classmates to write the body of your narrative paragraph on a separate piece of paper.

Name(s): _____

Word Connotations

Connotation has to do with the emotions we attach to the meaning of a word and the way it is used. Another way to think of this is to consider the ideas, mental pictures, or feelings we associate with particular words. Choose words carefully to make sure your readers understand exactly what you intend to say. When describing narrative experiences related to our topic for this unit, focus on positive connotations to engage readers.

1. Share the sentences you wrote on "Helping Hands" with a partner.

2. Highlight words that stand out to you in your partner's sentences.

3. Write each word on the top line of a separate box.

4. What other words, ideas, mental pictures, or emotions do you associate with each word? Write your thoughts about each word on the lines in its box.

Transition Words

➤ Objective

Students will identify transition words and phrases in sample paragraphs and generate lists of such words with partners. Then they will review their sentences and revise their writing to include appropriate transition words and phrases.

➤ Introduction

You will read narrative examples and think about how the authors used transition words and phrases to show shifts in time or location. Then you will create a word box of such words and compare notes with a partner. You will review sentences from your narrative paragraph and add transition words from your word box to make your writing flow more smoothly.

➤ Instruction

We use transition words to help guide readers through the actions in a narrative event. Not every sentence needs a transition word. The important thing is that the narrative flows naturally. In a narrative, transition words or phrases give readers a sense of time, since the actions that happen within an experience are usually described in chronological order. They may also explain location or provide illustrations or cause and effect.

➤ Guided Practice

Distribute "Getting Around My Narrative" (page 119). *Read one or more sample narrative paragraphs, for example, those from previous lessons or from classroom resources. Circle the transition words and phrases you notice in the sample. Which words and phrases indicate a shift in time frame or from one setting to another? How do transition words and phrases help the writing flow more smoothly? Write the words and phrases you notice in the word box in Part One. Discuss your findings with a partner and add any transition words you learn from your partner to your word box.*

➤ Independent Practice

Review the sentences you have written for your narrative paragraph. Circle words in the box you have already used in your sentences. In which places in your writing could you add a transition word or phrase to make your writing easier to read and understand? Revise your sentences and/or write new sentences for your paragraph, including transition words and phrases to show the passage of time or changes in location within the experience.

➤ Review

Provide examples of narrative paragraphs from classroom resources as necessary. Discuss how transition words and phrases make writing flow more smoothly and aid in reader comprehension.

➤ Closing

You located transition words and phrases in sample paragraphs and created a word box to use as a reference for your own writing. Then you reviewed sentences from your paragraph and revised them to include appropriate transition words to guide readers through your narrative.

Name(s): _____

Getting Around My Narrative

➤ Part One

1. Read one or more sample narrative paragraphs, for example, those from previous lessons or from classroom resources.

2. Circle the transition words and phrases you notice in the sample.

   - Which words and phrases indicate a shift in time frame or from one setting to another?

     _____

     _____

     _____

   - How do transition words and phrases help the writing flow more smoothly?

     _____

     _____

     _____

3. Write the words and phrases you notice in the word box below.

   ┌───┐
   │   │
   │   │
   │   │
   │   │
   │   │
   │   │
   └───┘

4. Discuss your findings with a partner.

5. Add any transition words you learn from your partner to your word box.

➤ Part Two

1. Review the sentences you have written for your narrative paragraph.

2. Circle words in the box you have already used in your sentences.

3. In which places in your writing could you add a transition word or phrase to make your writing easier to read and understand? Revise your sentences and/or write new sentences for your paragraph, including transition words and phrases to show the passage of time or changes in location within the experience. Use a separate piece of paper.

Concluding Sentences

➤ Objective

Students will read sample narrative paragraphs and write concluding sentences for each one. Then they will discuss their sentences to consider what makes a satisfactory ending for a narrative. They will also work in small groups to answer and discuss questions related to writing a concluding sentence that is relevant for readers and then write concluding sentences for their own paragraphs.

➤ Introduction

You will read sample narrative paragraphs and write a concluding sentence for each. Then you will discuss as a class what makes a satisfactory ending for a narrative, using your sample sentences as examples. You will also work with a small group to complete a graphic organizer about relevant concluding sentences and then write a concluding sentence for your narrative paragraph.

➤ Instruction

The concluding sentence of a narrative paragraph wraps up the experience. It flows naturally from the narrated experience in a logical way. Often the author will reflect on the impact of the experience and what he or she learned. After you've written most of your narrative, you might ask yourself, "So what? Why did I choose to write about this experience, and why would readers want to read about it?"

➤ Guided Practice

Display and distribute "A Satisfactory Conclusion" (page 121). *Read the two sample narratives and write a concluding sentence for each on separate slips of paper, labeling each sentence Paragraph A or Paragraph B.* Gather students' slips of paper to read samples aloud anonymously. *Which of these concluding statements provide an appropriate conclusion for the narrative described in Paragraph A? Why?* Discuss. *Which concluding statements provide a satisfactory ending for the narrative described in Paragraph B? Why?* Discuss.

➤ Independent Practice

Distribute "Making a Difference" (page 122). *Work with two other classmates in a triad to discuss the questions on the graphic organizer. Write your responses and the ideas you hear from your classmates. Review the sentences you have written for your paragraph on "Helping Hands" (page 116), "Word Connotations" (page 117), and "Getting Around My Narrative" (page 119). Read the notes you took on "Making a Difference" and consider your answers to the questions specifically in relation to your narrative experience. Then write a concluding sentence for your paragraph.*

➤ Review

Review students' responses to the questions on "Making a Difference" and discuss possible reasons readers might want to read about students' volunteer experiences and how they can make those experiences relevant for readers.

➤ Closing

You wrote sample concluding sentences for narrative paragraphs and discussed what makes a concluding sentence a satisfactory ending for a narrative experience. You discussed with classmates how a concluding sentence can leave readers with a sense of purpose and relevance and then wrote a concluding sentence for your narrative paragraph.

A Satisfactory Conclusion

Read the two sample narratives below and write a concluding sentence for each on a separate slip of paper. Label your sentences Paragraph A or Paragraph B as appropriate. Consider the following questions as you think about the best way to end the narrative:

- How might this experience end?
- What would follow naturally from what has already been narrated?
- What is the impact of this experience on the narrator or main character?
- Why did the author choose to write about this experience?
- Why would readers want to read about this experience?
- How is the experience relevant for readers?

➤ Paragraph A: Community Service

Last week, my friends and I planned a gathering to work together on our community service project. Students at our school are required to do one project per term. We are allowed to choose what we want to do, as long as we have the teacher's approval. My friends had several ideas, but finally we decided to write letters to veterans and people still serving in the military. Our school has access to a program that delivers the letters. It also provides guidelines for us for our protection as well as those receiving the letters. One of my friends has an uncle serving in the military. She suggested we pretend we were writing to someone we knew, although we would have to follow the guidelines for topics of conversation. At first, I had trouble getting started, but then it got easier as I remembered to think of the other person.

> **Teacher Notes**
>
> Grade level: appropriate
> Lexile estimate: 1020L

➤ Paragraph B: Classroom Buddies

I eagerly anticipated my opportunity to volunteer at the day-care center next door to our school. As part of a "buddy" program, my class would visit with the preschool children who attended the center. As we walked down the hall to the preschool room, toddler cries and whimpers mingled with children's chatter. I wondered what we had in store for us. Our teacher introduced us to Wanda, the preschool teacher. A small boy gripped Wanda's hand with one fist and sucked the thumb of his other hand. Wanda gave us a tour of the classroom, including where to find paper towels and tissues, activities we could do with the children, and most importantly, where the animal crackers were kept. I could only imagine the significance of those. A toddler arrived and, as her parent left to go to work, she began to cry, although I would describe it as more of a howl. Wanda was busy with another child, so I tried to distract the little girl with a musical toy, then a soft puppy stuffed animal, but nothing seemed to work. "Give her an animal cracker," Wanda said. I rushed to the giant jar and pulled it down. As soon as the toddler heard the scraping of the lid being twisted off, her wailing subsided. "Want a cookie?" I asked her, and she sniffed and nodded.

> **Teacher Notes**
>
> Grade level: below
> Lexile estimate: 920L

Name(s): _____

Making a Difference

Work with two other classmates in a triad to discuss the questions on the graphic organizer below. Think about your specific narrative experience as you write responses and the ideas you hear from your classmates.

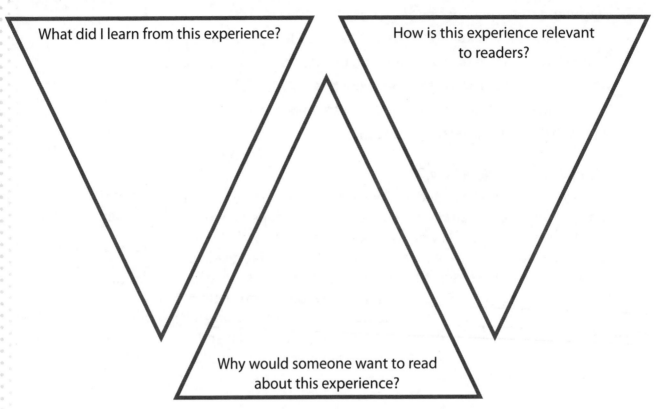

What did I learn from this experience?

How is this experience relevant to readers?

Why would someone want to read about this experience?

Review the sentences you have written for your paragraph on "Helping Hands" (page 116), "Word Connotations" (page 117), and "Getting Around My Narrative" (page 119). Read the notes you took and then write a concluding sentence for your paragraph.

_____

_____

_____

_____

First Draft and Peer Review

➤ Objective

Students will use their notes from previous activities in this module to write first drafts of their narrative paragraphs and post them to the class blog (if available). Then they will read and comment on classmates' paragraphs and share their feedback in small writing critique groups.

➤ Introduction

You will use your notes and writing from previous activities in this module to write a first draft of your narrative paragraph. Then you will read classmates' narrative paragraphs and write constructive comments for each paragraph you read. You will share your feedback with a small writing critique group.

➤ Instruction

Often when we are ready to write a first draft, we already have an outline or notes about what we want to include in the narrative. You may need to brainstorm additional ideas and details about the topic or the volunteer experience you will describe. Use vivid descriptions to involve readers in the experience. Be sure to include an introductory sentence that orients readers to the situation and captures their attention. End your paragraph with an effective concluding sentence that refers to the significance or impact of the narrated event or experience.

➤ Guided Practice

Use your notes and writing from "Introduce a Character" (page 112), "Orient Readers" (page 113), "Actions Within the Experience" (page 114), "Helping Hands" (page 116), and "Word Connotations" (page 117) to write sentences for your first draft. Refer to your notes from "Getting Around My Narrative" (page 119) to include transition words to guide readers through your writing. Finish with your concluding sentence from "Making a Difference" (page 122). If possible, establish a class blog for students to post their first drafts. *Post your first draft to the class blog.*

➤ Independent Practice

Distribute "My Writing Group" (page 124), one copy for each paragraph students will review (keep student critique groups to no more than three or four students). *Members of a writing critique group analyze and evaluate one another's writing. They also comment and offer constructive feedback to each other. Access the first drafts of your small-group members' narrative paragraphs or read print copies. Read a classmate's narrative paragraph. Then follow the guidelines on your activity page to write constructive feedback about your classmate's writing. Complete one page for each member of your writing group.*

➤ Review

Model how to give and receive constructive feedback graciously. Together as a class, discuss the feedback students received from their peers. What could they do to give and receive more accurate feedback?

➤ Closing

You wrote a first draft of your narrative paragraph today. Then you gave and received feedback on your writing with others in a small writing group.

Name(s): _____

My Writing Group

Read a classmate's narrative paragraph. Use the following prompts to write constructive feedback about your classmate's writing on the lines below. Complete one page for each paragraph you read.

- Say what you appreciate about the writing.
- Ask questions about the work.
- Offer specific suggestions for improvement.
- Give your honest evaluation of your classmate's effort.
- Receive feedback about your writing from a classmate graciously.
- Apply new information to your own writing.

As you write comments for a classmate, keep these friendly tips in mind.

- Be kind.
- Be helpful.

- Be honest.
- Show respect.

- Be fair.
- Be caring.

_____

_____

_____

_____

_____

_____

_____

_____

_____

_____

_____

_____

_____

_____

_____

_____

_____

Second Draft and Self-Evaluation

➤ Objective

Students will work with partners to list characteristics of narrative writing. Then they will use their notes to revise their first drafts and write second drafts of their narrative paragraphs. They will evaluate their second drafts using a rubric and answer questions about their next steps in the writing process.

➤ Introduction

Today you will review and list characteristics of effective narrative writing with a partner. Then you will make revision notes on your first draft and write a second draft of your narrative paragraph. You will also use a rubric to evaluate your second draft.

➤ Instruction

The second draft gives writers the opportunity to continue to revise and make their writing stronger. One way to strengthen writing is to check grammar and sentence structure. Make sure sentences start in a variety of ways. This keeps your writing interesting for readers. Check for concrete words: Does your writing have specific nouns that show readers exactly what you are writing about? Do you use precise adjectives to describe the nouns? Do you use pronouns and verbs correctly?

➤ Guided Practice

Work with a partner to list characteristics of effective narrative writing. Use your list to discuss and note possible revisions to your first draft to strengthen your writing. Then review the feedback you received on "My Writing Group" (page 124) to make additional notes on your first draft and write a second draft of your narrative paragraph.

➤ Independent Practice

Distribute "Self-Evaluation: Narrative Paragraph" (page 126) and highlighters. *According to this rubric, what are the characteristics of effective narrative writing? How closely do your criteria match the descriptions of effective narrative writing on this rubric? Read the descriptions of the different levels of quality for each category. Then use the rubric to evaluate your narrative paragraph. Highlight or circle the description for each part of a narrative paragraph that matches your writing. Take your evaluation another step by answering these questions on a separate piece of paper: What did I learn from this evaluation? What action(s) will I take next to strengthen my writing? What questions do I have about how to do this? Share your responses to your questions with your partner.*

➤ Review

Discuss the impact revising has on the writing process. Review specific categories of the rubric, as needed, to guide students as they write their second drafts.

➤ Closing

You created a list of characteristics of effective narrative writing to revise and write a second draft of your narrative paragraph. Then you used a rubric to evaluate your writing and consider the next steps you will take in the writing process.

Self-Evaluation: Narrative Paragraph

Name: _____   Score: _____

	4	3	2	1
Beginning Sentence	My narrative has a beginning sentence that introduces a narrator and/or characters, a setting, and a volunteer experience to orient readers.	My narrative has a sentence that introduces a narrator, a setting, and an experience with volunteering.	My narrative has a sentence that introduces a character who narrates an experience.	My narrative does not have a sentence that introduces the narrator, characters, setting, or experience.
Experience/ Event	My narrator describes a volunteer experience in an order that makes sense.	My narrator describes a volunteer experience.	My narrator describes an experience, but it is not told in an order that makes sense.	My narrative does not describe an experience.
Descriptive Words and Actions	I use description and action to describe the volunteer experience and to show how characters respond.	I use description and action to describe the volunteer experience.	I use action or description to describe an experience.	I do not use action or description adequately to describe an experience.
Details	I include concrete words and sensory details to describe a volunteer experience.	I include concrete words or sensory details to describe a volunteer experience.	I include details to describe an experience.	I do not include specific details to describe an experience.
Transition Words	I use transition words and phrases to guide readers through a logical sequence of actions within the experience.	I use transition words in some places to show the order of actions within the experience.	I use transition words once or twice to show the order of actions within the experience.	I do not use transition words to show the order of actions within the experience.
Concluding Sentence	My narrative has a concluding sentence that flows naturally from the narrated experience and provides a sense of closure.	My narrative has a concluding sentence that describes the end of the experience.	My narrative has a concluding sentence.	My narrative does not have a concluding sentence.

Final Draft

➤ Objective

Students will reflect on their purpose for writing and identify possible audiences for their narratives. They will randomly select audiences to discuss with classmates. Then they will use their self-evaluation scores and revision notes to produce final copies of their narrative paragraphs.

➤ Introduction

You will write a paragraph to reflect on your purpose for writing and also identify possible audiences for your narrative. Then you will discuss these options with classmates. You will also use your self-evaluation scores and revision notes to write a final draft of your narrative paragraph.

➤ Instruction

The final draft of a narrative piece is the copy we will present to an audience. We want our writing to be as clear as possible to make it easy for readers to understand. Think about the experience your narrative describes. Are there any gaps in your narrative? Add any further details needed to bring the experience to life for readers. Make sure the actions within the experience follow each other in a logical order. Who would most enjoy reading about this experience? How will you connect your writing with your audience? A final draft represents writing that has been strengthened and improved through multiple revisions.

➤ Guided Practice

Distribute "Grab Your Audience" (page 128) and students' copies of "Making a Difference" (page 122). *Refer to your notes on the graphic organizer to write a paragraph about your purpose for writing about this particular experience. Who might be a potential audience for your writing? Identify one or more people or groups of people who would want to read about your experience. Write one potential audience on each bag. Select one option at random to share with a partner. Then ask your partner how appropriate or relevant that audience would be for his or her writing and why. As time allows, select another random option and discuss it with a different classmate.*

➤ Independent Practice

Review the scores you gave your second draft on "Self-Evaluation: Narrative Paragraph" (page 126) and your answers to the evaluation questions. Use your notes to write or type a final draft of your narrative paragraph with your audience in mind.

➤ Review

Review with students possible authentic audiences for their narrative writing and how they might connect their writing with their chosen audiences. Provide technology resources for students to produce their final copies.

➤ Closing

You identified an audience for your narrative paragraph and used your self-evaluation scores and revision notes to produce a final copy.

Name(s): _____

Grab Your Audience

1. What was your purpose in writing this narrative paragraph? Refer to your notes on "Making a Difference" (page 122) to write a paragraph about your purpose for writing about this particular experience.

_____

_____

_____

_____

_____

_____

_____

_____

2. Who might be a potential audience for your writing? Identify one or more people or groups of people who would want to read about your experience. Write one potential audience on each bag.

3. Select one option at random to share with a partner. Ask your partner how appropriate or relevant that audience would be for his or her writing and why.

Final Evaluation

➤ Objective

Students will record their scores from their self-evaluations and teacher evaluations to compare their performance in specific aspects of narrative writing. Then they will write what they have learned and set goals to strengthen their writing in the next module.

➤ Introduction

You will compare the scores you gave your narrative paragraph on your self-evaluation with the scores you received from me on a teacher evaluation. Then you will use your observations to write what you have learned about your narrative writing regarding specific characteristics. You will also set goals to strengthen your writing in the next module.

➤ Instruction

When you compare your own self-evaluation with the scores you receive from me, you are comparing data in the same categories (characteristics of effective narrative writing) from different sources. Reflecting on the similarities and differences in the scores provides information that helps us set goals for strengthening our writing in specific characteristics of narrative writing.

➤ Guided Practice

Distribute "Steps Toward Mastery" (page 131), various colored pencils, and students' copies of "Self-Evaluation: Narrative Paragraph" (page 126) and "Teacher Evaluation: Narrative Paragraph" (page 130). *According to the rubric, which qualities describe excellent narrative writing? Discuss as a class. Think about the qualities we discussed together as a class. Reflect on the questions listed and write your thoughts on a separate piece of paper. Then record the scores from "Self-Evaluation: Narrative Paragraph" on the corresponding steps of the diagram. With a different-colored pencil, record your scores from "Teacher Evaluation: Narrative Paragraph."*

➤ Independent Practice

Based on the scores you recorded, what will be your next steps toward excellent narrative writing? What have you learned about specific aspects of narrative writing from these evaluations? Think about each characteristic and write what you have learned on the relevant "steps" or a separate piece of paper. What goal(s) do you have for your narrative writing?

Select one or more aspects of narrative writing as a focus for strengthening your writing during the next module: writing a narrative essay. Write your goal(s) on the appropriate "steps" or a separate piece of paper.

➤ Review

Model how to reflect on score comparisons for each category of the rubric to assess learning. Discuss possible goals students might set for their writing as they look ahead to the next module.

➤ Closing

You used a step diagram to compare the scores you gave your writing on a self-evaluation with the scores you received from me. You also wrote what you learned about various aspects of your narrative writing and set goals to strengthen your writing as you write a narrative essay in the next module.

Teacher Evaluation: Narrative Paragraph

Student Name: _____ **Score:** _____

	4	3	2	1
Beginning Sentence	The narrative has a beginning sentence that introduces a narrator and/or characters, a setting, and a volunteer experience to orient readers.	The narrative has a sentence that introduces a narrator, a setting, and an experience with volunteering.	The narrative has a sentence that introduces a character who narrates an experience.	The narrative does not have a beginning sentence that introduces the narrator, characters, setting, or experience.
Experience/ Event	The narrator describes a volunteer experience in an order that makes sense.	The narrator describes a volunteer experience.	The narrator describes an experience, but it is not told in an order that makes sense.	The narrative does not describe an experience.
Descriptive Words and Actions	The author uses description and action to describe the volunteer experience and to show how characters respond.	The author uses description and action to describe the volunteer experience.	The author uses action or description to describe an experience.	The author does not use action or description adequately to describe an experience.
Details	The author includes concrete words and sensory details to describe a volunteer experience.	The author includes concrete words or sensory details to describe a volunteer experience.	The author includes details to describe an experience.	The author does not include specific details to describe an experience.
Transition Words	The author uses transition words and phrases to guide readers through a logical sequence of actions within the experience.	The author uses transition words in some places to show the order of actions within the experience.	The author uses transition words once or twice to show the order of actions within the experience.	The author does not use transition words to show the order of actions within the experience.
Concluding Sentence	The narrative has a concluding sentence that flows naturally from the narrated experience and provides a sense of closure.	The narrative has a concluding sentence that describes the end of the experience.	The narrative has a concluding sentence.	The narrative does not have a concluding sentence.

Name(s): _____

Steps Toward Mastery

1. Record your scores from "Self-Evaluation: Narrative Paragraph" (page 126) on the corresponding steps below.

2. With a different-colored pencil, record your scores from "Teacher Evaluation: Narrative Paragraph" (page 130).

3. According to the rubric, which qualities describe mastery of narrative writing? Think about the qualities you discussed together as a class. Reflect on the questions listed below and write your thoughts on a separate piece of paper.
   - What next step will you take toward mastering narrative writing?
   - What have you learned about specific aspects of narrative writing from these evaluations?
   - What goal(s) do you have for your narrative writing?
   - What next step will you take to develop mastery in your narrative writing skills?

4. Think about each characteristic and write what you have learned on the relevant "steps" or a separate piece of paper.

5. Select one or more aspects of narrative writing as a focus for strengthening your writing during the next module: writing a narrative essay. Write your goal(s) on the appropriate "step(s)" or a separate piece of paper.

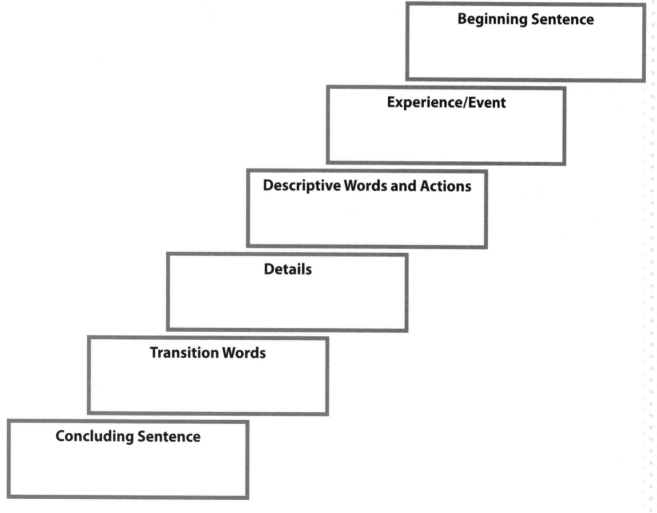

Beginning Sentence

Experience/Event

Descriptive Words and Actions

Details

Transition Words

Concluding Sentence

Review

➤ Objective

Students will read a sample paragraph and then work with partners to list characteristics of narrative writing they notice in the paragraph. Then they will write definitions of effective narrative writing based on what they have learned during this module.

➤ Introduction

Today you will read a sample narrative paragraph and list characteristics of narrative writing you notice in the paragraph. Then you will write your own definition of effective narrative writing.

➤ Instruction

Narrative writing describes a real or imagined experience by conveying a clear sequence of events with descriptive details and action. It has an opening sentence that introduces a narrator and establishes a setting and context for the story. Concrete words and sensory details invite readers to experience the actions of the experience along with the narrator. It has transitions that indicate the passage of time and guide readers through the experience. A satisfactory concluding sentence ends the experience in a way that makes sense based on the actions that happened.

➤ Guided Practice

Distribute "Define Narrative Writing" (page 134) and "Students Helping Students" (page 133). *Read the sample narrative paragraph with a partner. Then work together to list the characteristics of narrative writing you notice in the paragraph. What are the strengths of the paragraph? Which aspects of the paragraph would you change to make it more effective? Write your changes at the end of Part One.*

➤ Independent Practice

Based on the characteristics you listed with a classmate, how would you define narrative writing for someone else? Write your description of narrative writing in Part Two of "Define Narrative Writing."

➤ Review

Review characteristics of effective narrative writing described on "Teacher Evaluation: Narrative Paragraph" (page 130) and go over the sample paragraph with students as needed. As time allows, invite students to share their definitions of narrative writing.

➤ Closing

You identified characteristics of narrative writing demonstrated in a sample paragraph and created a list. Then you wrote your own definition of narrative writing to review what you have learned.

Students Helping Students

Where I live it rains a tremendous amount. However, yesterday in current events, we read about a city that is flooded from a severe storm. In class, we discussed how we could volunteer to help students who were affected by the storm. One idea was to have a fundraiser to earn money that we could donate to the cause. We decided while that would be practical, it didn't feel very caring and personal. Mr. Sanderson mentioned that we could purchase new school supplies to help students and their families. We worked

together to create a master shopping list with items such as pens and pencils, notebooks, erasers, and markers. In addition, we suggested titles of books our class likes in our school library. Our teacher reminded us that all books and other supplies had to be purchased new. Then we worked in small groups to break the list down and make individual assignments. We based the list on what each person would be able to contribute so that everyone in the class could participate. One student might purchase a paperback copy of a novel, and another person might donate a single notebook. For those who couldn't participate for financial reasons, Mr. Sanderson suggested they form a team to prepare the items for shipping. All of us felt fortunate to be safe and healthy and in a position to volunteer and help others.

Teacher Notes

Grade level: appropriate
Lexile estimate: 1020L

Name(s): _____

Define Narrative Writing

➤ Part One

Read "Students Helping Students" (page 133) with a partner. Work together to list the characteristics of narrative writing you notice in the paragraph.

- _____
  _____
- _____
  _____
- _____
  _____
- _____
  _____
- _____
  _____
- _____

What are the strengths of the paragraph?

_____

_____

Which aspects of the paragraph would you change to make it more effective?

_____

_____

_____

➤ Part Two

How would you define narrative writing for someone else? Write your description of narrative writing below.

_____

_____

_____

Introductory Paragraphs

➤ Objective

Students will discuss story archetypes and practice creating story arcs for known stories then create arcs for their own narrative experiences. They will also write sample sentences to introduce their narrative essays.

➤ Introduction

You will discuss story archetypes with a partner and then practice completing a story arc for your narrative essay. You will also follow specific suggestions to practice writing thesis statements for your essay. Our topic for this module is nanotechnology.

➤ Instruction

In the introductory paragraph of a narrative, authors introduce the setting and context of the situation, including the narrator and characters involved. It is important to introduce the story in an interesting way to catch readers' attention, so they will want to keep reading. The hook, or first sentence, may cause readers to ask questions about the narrative. In a narrative essay, the thesis statement introduces the action that is part of the experience.

➤ Guided Practice

Distribute "Planning My Narrative" (page 136). *Many stories we experience, such as those in books and movies, follow an "archetype." An archetype is an example or typical situation that might happen in a story. Discuss the listed archetypes with a partner, draw a star by those you recognize, and give an example of a book or movie that follows that general storyline. With your partner, choose one story type and complete a general story arc for it. What happens first to engage readers and draw them into the story situation? Write the opening of the story at the left side of the arc. Write one thing that happens—an obstacle or point of conflict the main character faces—in the middle of the arc. Write how the story ends at the right side of the arc. On a separate piece of paper, create a similar arc for the narrative experience you plan to describe.*

➤ Independent Practice

Distribute "Engage Readers" (page 137). *Nanotechnology focuses on minute details and manipulates individual molecules. Similarly, authors introduce specific details of narratives in the introductory paragraph. Focus on a few key areas to orient readers at the beginning of your narrative. Below each magnifying glass in Part One, write a sample sentence to introduce that aspect of your narrative. Then use your notes from Part One and the ideas listed in Part Two to experiment with writing sample thesis statements for your narrative essay on a separate piece of paper.*

➤ Review

Review examples of different types of thesis statements from sample narrative essays. As time allows, generate sample thesis statements together as a class on the topic for this module.

➤ Closing

You discussed story archetypes and created a story arc for your narrative. Then you practiced writing thesis statements for your essay based on suggested ideas.

Name(s): _____

Planning My Narrative

Many stories we experience, such as those in books and movies, follow an "archetype." An archetype is an example or typical situation that might happen in a story.

1. Discuss the following archetypes with a partner and draw a star by those you recognize. Then give an example of a book or movie that follows that general storyline.

> Rags to riches: _____
>
> The quest: _____
>
> Coming of age: _____
>
> Good versus evil: _____
>
> Fall from grace: _____
>
> Voyage and return: _____
>
> Overcoming a monster: _____

2. With your partner, choose one story type and complete a general story arc for it.

    • What happens first to engage readers and draw them into the story situation? Write the opening of the story at the left side of the arc below.

    • Write one thing that happens—an obstacle or point of conflict the main character faces— in the middle of the arc.

    • Write how the story ends at the right side of the arc.

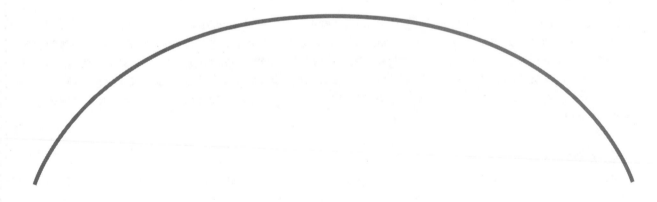

3. On a separate piece of paper, create a similar arc for the narrative experience you plan to describe.

Name(s): _____

Engage Readers

➤ Part One

Nanotechnology focuses on minute details and manipulates individual molecules. Similarly, authors introduce specific details of narratives in the introductory paragraph. Focus on a few key areas to orient readers at the beginning of your narrative. Below each magnifying glass, write a sample sentence to introduce that aspect of your narrative.

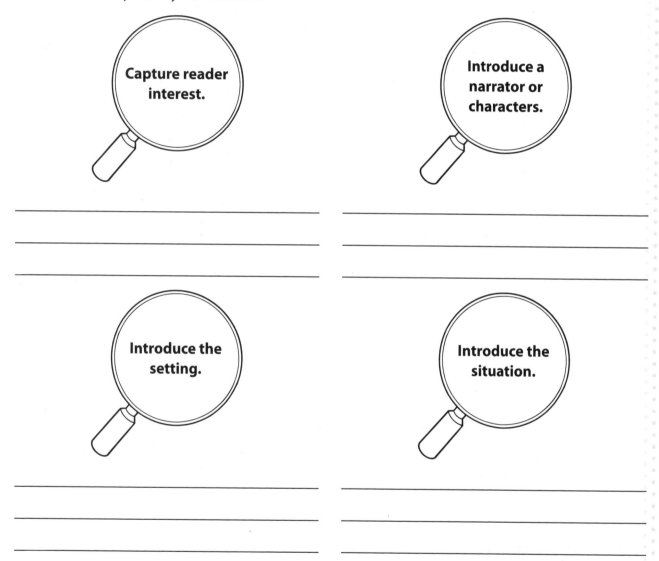

Capture reader interest.

Introduce a narrator or characters.

Introduce the setting.

Introduce the situation.

➤ Part Two

Use your notes from Part One and the ideas listed below to experiment with writing sample thesis statements for your narrative essay on a separate piece of paper.

- Introduce readers to the who, what, where, when, and why of the narrative.
- Preview a lesson learned.
- Condense the main ideas into one or two concepts to offer a hint of a theme.
- Write an engaging "hook" to capture reader interest.

Body Paragraphs

➤ Objective

Students will work in small groups to describe details about a particular aspect of a narrative experience. They will also write action sentences for their narratives and give and receive feedback with partners to add appropriate transition words and phrases. Then they will write dialogue with partners to accompany the actions in their narrative sentences.

➤ Introduction

You will work with a small group to brainstorm and write sensory descriptive words to describe details of a setting or event of a narrative experience. Then you will use clues from another group to guess the detail they described. You will write action sentences for your narrative and discuss transitions with a partner. You will then write dialogue to go along with the actions in your sentences.

➤ Instruction

People respond in different ways to things that happen to them. Characters react by talking or acting. Authors use dialogue and concrete words to show speech and action in a narrative. Descriptive words that involve the senses help readers envision the details of the setting and event. Authors use transition words in narratives to show the passage of time. Transitions can also show characters moving from one place to another. These words and phrases help to organize events in an experience so that readers can follow the action.

➤ Guided Practice

Distribute "Describing an Experience" (page 139). *Work with a small group to brainstorm and list details (people, places, objects) that might be part of a narrative experience. Choose one detail to describe as a group. Complete the chart as you consider the listed questions. Write concrete, sensory words to describe the detail. Then share your descriptive words with another small group as clues without identifying the detail described. Have the other group guess your group's detail.*

➤ Independent Practice

Distribute "Actions and Reactions" (page 140). *Refer to your notes from "Planning My Narrative" (page 136) and the thesis statement(s) you wrote on "Engage Readers" (page 137) to think about what happens in your narrative. Use the questions in Part One as prompts to write your way through a body paragraph of your narrative. Then discuss what you learned about transition words on "Getting Around My Narrative" (from Module 5, page 119) with a partner. Read the sentences you wrote in Part One to a partner and ask him or her to listen for places where transition words would make the writing easier to understand. Add transition words and phrases to your writing as appropriate.*

Distribute "My Response Is . . ." (page 141). *In Part One, review the characters' actions and events that happen as part of your narrative experience. What are characters saying during the experience? With a partner, take turns writing dialogue in reaction to something your characters say. Write something a character says in the first speech bubble on the left. Trade papers with your partner and ask him or her to write what he or she would say in response to your character's dialogue. Your partner will write his or her response in the speech bubble on the right. Write something else a character says in the second speech bubble on the left, and so on. Discuss the questions in Part Two with your partner to think about the role of dialogue in narrative writing.*

➤ Review

Review examples of dialogue that add to an experience and show part of the character's actions, thoughts, or feelings in the narrative.

➤ Closing

You worked with a small group to practice writing descriptive words to show details in a narrative. Then you wrote action sentences for your narrative and worked with a partner to include transition words and phrases. You also wrote dialogue to go along with your characters' actions.

Describing an Experience

1. Work with a small group to brainstorm and list details (e.g., people, places, objects) that might be part of a narrative experience.

2. Choose one detail to describe as a group.

3. Complete the chart as you consider the questions below. Write concrete, sensory words to describe the detail.

   - How does this detail affect the character(s)?
   - How do characters interact with this detail?
   - How do characters react to this detail?

Our group will describe _____.

What Characters See	What Characters Hear
What Characters Touch/How It Feels to the Touch	**What Characters Smell**
What Characters Think	**What Characters Feel**

4. Share your descriptive words with another small group as clues without identifying the detail described.

5. Have them use the clues to guess the detail your group chose.

Name(s): _____

Actions and Reactions

➤ Part One

1. Refer to your notes from "Planning My Narrative" (page 136) and the thesis statement(s) you wrote on "Engage Readers" (page 137) to think about what happens in your narrative.

2. Think of the questions below as prompts to write your way through a body paragraph of your narrative. This paragraph will show a sequence of actions that are part of one event in the narrative experience.

3. Consider actions as you write one sentence about your narrative experience to answer each question.

- What does the character want?

  _____

- What obstacle or conflict gets in the way of that goal?

  _____

- What happens to the character as he or she perseveres to get what he or she wants?

  _____

- How does the character react to what happens?

  _____

- What question or problem does the character face as a result of his or her action?

  _____

- What does the character decide to do next?

  _____

- How does the character react to this situation?

  _____

➤ Part Two

1. With a partner, discuss what you learned about transition words on "Getting Around My Narrative" (from Module 5, page 119).

2. Read the sentences you wrote in Part One of this activity to a partner and ask him or her to listen for places where transition words would make the writing easier to understand.

3. Add transition words and phrases to your writing as appropriate.

Name(s): _____

My Response Is . . .

➤ Part One

1. Review the characters' actions and events that happen as part of your narrative experience. What are characters saying during the experience?

2. With a partner, take turns writing dialogue in reaction to something your characters say. Write something a character says in the first speech bubble on the left.

3. Trade papers with your partner and ask him or her to write what he or she would say in response to your character's dialogue. Your partner will write his or her response in the speech bubble on the right.

4. Write something else a character says in the second speech bubble on the left. Ask your partner to write his or her response to this new piece of dialogue in the second speech bubble on the right.

5. Continue in the same way for the third set of speech bubbles.

➤ Part Two

Discuss the following questions:

- How does dialogue help move a story forward?
- How can you use dialogue to show what happens in a narrative experience instead of telling readers what happened?

Conclusions

➤ Objective

Students will complete a diagram to consider the significance of their narratives and how they can connect to readers. They will give and receive oral feedback with partners. Then they will write conclusions for their narratives and complete comment forms for partners.

➤ Introduction

You will reflect on the main idea of your narrative essay to consider the significance of the experience and make connections with your readers. Then you will write a conclusion for your essay and exchange comments with a partner.

➤ Instruction

Effective narrative writing gives readers a powerful emotional experience. This means what happened to the characters in the narrative influences the reader in some way. The conclusion in a narrative essay brings the experience to a close. Allow readers to come to their own conclusions. The author may reflect on how this experience changed the way he or she thinks or will do things in the future. Alternatively, the ending of a narrative essay may impact readers in some way with a thought to ponder or a lesson learned from the experience.

➤ Guided Practice

Distribute "Connect to Readers" (page 143). *Write the main idea from your thesis statement in the center oval. Consider the connections you can make as a result of this experience. Then answer each of the questions in the boxes in Part One.*

Complete Part Two by sharing your completed diagram with a partner. Ask for feedback to strengthen your conclusion. Take notes on your partner's comments on the back of the page or on a separate piece of paper.

➤ Independent Practice

Distribute "A Meaningful Conclusion" (page 144). *Use your ideas from "Connect to Readers" and the feedback you received to write a conclusion for your narrative essay on a separate piece of paper. Then trade papers with a partner and ask him or her to read your conclusion. Complete the comment form to help your partner identify characteristics of an effective conclusion in his or her writing. As you provide feedback to your partner, remember to write kind, honest, and helpful comments.*

➤ Review

Model how to condense the main idea or theme from a thesis statement for the center oval of the diagram on "Connect to Readers" to clarify, as necessary.

➤ Closing

You completed a diagram to think about the significance of your narrative experience and how you might connect with your readers. Then you wrote the conclusion for your essay and exchanged comments with a partner to strengthen your writing.

Name(s): _____

Connect to Readers

➤ Part One

- Write the main idea from your thesis statement in the center oval.
- Consider the connections you can make as a result of this experience. Then answer each of the questions in the boxes.

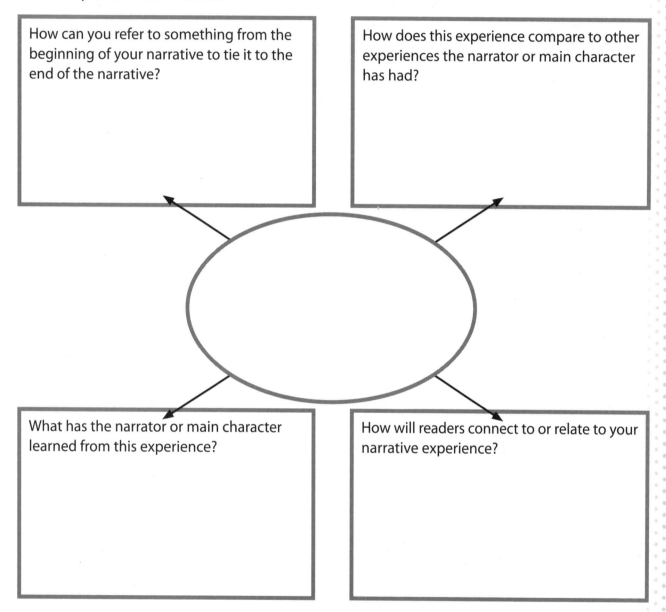

How can you refer to something from the beginning of your narrative to tie it to the end of the narrative?

How does this experience compare to other experiences the narrator or main character has had?

What has the narrator or main character learned from this experience?

How will readers connect to or relate to your narrative experience?

➤ Part Two

- Share your completed diagram with a partner.
- Ask for feedback to strengthen your conclusion.
- Take notes on your partner's comments on the back of this page or on a separate piece of paper.

Name(s): _____

A Meaningful Conclusion

1. Use your ideas from "Connect to Readers" (page 143) and the feedback you received to write a conclusion for your narrative essay on a separate piece of paper.

2. Trade your conclusion and this page with a partner.

3. Ask your partner to read your conclusion and then complete the comment form below.

Your Partner's Conclusion	My Comments
How did the conclusion bring the narrative experience to a close?	
How did what happened to the characters influence me?	
What conclusions did I come to about the experience?	
How did the experience change the way the the narrator or main character thinks or will do things in the future?	
What did the the narrator or main character learn from the experience?	
What did I learn from reading this narrative essay?	

First Draft and Peer Review

➤ Objective

Students will write first drafts of their narrative essays and review characteristics of effective narrative writing. They will review classmates' writing and use the feedback they receive to set goals for their own writing.

➤ Introduction

You will use your notes and writing from previous activities in this module to write a first draft of your narrative essay. Then you will review characteristics of effective narrative writing and review a partner's writing. You will use the feedback you receive to set goals for strengthening your writing.

➤ Instruction

When an author writes a first draft, he or she puts together all his or her notes and ideas into one complete narrative in order, from introductory paragraph to conclusion. In your first draft, you will put together your notes and practice sentences from activities in previous lessons to write your narrative essay. Your draft will include an introductory paragraph, in which you introduce a narrator, setting, and situation. The body paragraphs will describe the events that were part of the narrative experience, in the order they happened. Concrete words and sensory details should be used to describe the experience, and dialogue and actions will show how characters reacted to what happened. The conclusion will end the narrative in a way that makes sense and leaves readers with something to think about.

➤ Guided Practice

Review the introductory sentences and thesis statements you wrote on "Engage Readers" (page 137) to write an introductory paragraph. Did you include an interesting sentence to capture readers' attention? Refer to your story arc on "Planning My Narrative" (page 136) and your sentences from "Actions and Reactions" (page 140) to write one or more additional body paragraphs for your essay. Include descriptive words and dialogue such as those you wrote on "Describing an Experience" (page 139) and "My Response Is..." (page 141). Review your insights from "Connect to Readers" (page 143) and the feedback you received from classmates to revise and strengthen the conclusion you wrote on "A Meaningful Conclusion" (page 144).

➤ Independent Practice

Distribute "Setting Goals for Excellence" (page 146). *Review the list of characteristics of effective narrative writing with a partner. Read your partner's narrative essay and use the chart to assign a score to his or her writing for each listed narrative characteristic. In the box next to each characteristic, write the score you would give that aspect of your partner's essay. Then use the feedback you receive from your partner and the list of narrative characteristics to set goals for your writing. Refer to the diagram as a guide and write your goals on a separate piece of paper.*

➤ Review

If possible, provide examples of writing from various resources that demonstrate different levels of quality in narrative writing. Discuss the characteristics listed on "Setting Goals for Excellence" to clarify.

➤ Closing

You wrote a first draft of your narrative essay. Then you reviewed characteristics of effective narrative writing with a partner, gave and received feedback, and set goals for your writing.

Name(s): _____

Setting Goals for Excellence

1. Review the following list of characteristics of effective narrative writing with a partner.

    ☐ The narrative introduces a narrator and/or characters who had an experience with nanotechnology.

    ☐ The narrative introduces a setting and situation to orient readers.

    ☐ The narrator describes events in the experience in an order that makes sense.

    ☐ The narrative includes dialogue and description to show how characters respond to events within the experience.

    ☐ The author includes concrete words and sensory details to describe events in the narrative.

    ☐ Transition words and phrases guide readers through the sequence of events.

    ☐ The narrative has a conclusion that flows naturally from the narrated experience and provides a sense of closure.

2. Read your partner's narrative essay and use the chart below to assign a score to his or her writing for each narrative characteristic listed above. In the box next to each characteristic, write the score you would give that aspect of your partner's essay.

4	3	2	1
Writing meets this characteristic with excellence.	Writing meets this characteristic sufficiently.	Writing partially meets this characteristic.	Writing needs revision to meet this characteristic.

3. Use the feedback you receive from your partner and the list of narrative characteristics to set goals for your writing.

4. Refer to the diagram below as a guide and write your goals on a separate piece of paper.

My goals

What I will do to meet my goals

How I will know I've reached a goal

What I will do to celebrate my accomplishment

Second Draft and Self-Evaluation

➤ Objective

Students will use feedback they have received from a partner, revision notes, and goals they have set for their writing to write second drafts of their narrative essays. Then they will use a rubric to evaluate their second drafts and reflect on their writing progress.

➤ Introduction

You will use feedback you have received and any revision notes you have made to write a second draft of your narrative essay. Then you will use a rubric to evaluate your writing and reflect on your progress toward meeting the goals you set to strengthen and improve your writing.

➤ Instruction

Think about the qualities of effective narrative writing as you write the second draft of your narrative essay. Include specific descriptions of people, places, and things to give readers a mental picture of the experience. Use sensory details; for example, describe what a character sees, hears, or smells. Show readers what the character encounters and how they react to events in the experience. Consider using figurative language to make your writing more interesting. Check the progression of events in your narrative and fill in any gaps with details as needed.

➤ Guided Practice

Review the characteristics of narrative writing listed on "Setting Goals for Excellence" (page 146) and the feedback you received from your partner. Use any revision notes you wrote on your first draft and the goals you set for your writing to write a second draft of your narrative essay.

➤ Independent Practice

Distribute "Self-Evaluation: Narrative Essay" (page 148) and different-colored pencils or highlighters. *Evaluate your second draft using "Self-Evaluation: Narrative Essay." Circle or highlight the description for each part of a narrative essay that matches your writing. Review the goals you wrote during the "Setting Goals for Excellence" activity in the previous lesson. Use one color to underline or highlight parts of your essay that demonstrate progress toward meeting your goals. Use a different color to identify areas you would like to strengthen when you write your final draft and underline or highlight those sentences.*

➤ Review

Review "Self-Evaluation: Narrative Essay" with students and answer any questions about the rubric. Review correct punctuation for dialogue as needed. Discuss how students can use the characteristics described on the rubric to identify areas they would like to strengthen when they write their final drafts.

➤ Closing

You used a rubric to evaluate your second draft and considered strengths and weaknesses in your writing. Use the scores on your rubric and your notes to write a final draft of your narrative. Type your final copy if possible and bring it back to class for the next lesson.

Self-Evaluation: Narrative Essay

Name: _____   Score: _____

	4	**3**	**2**	**1**
Narrator and/ or Characters	My narrative introduces a narrator and/or characters who had an experience with nanotechnology.	My narrative introduces a narrator who had an experience with nanotechnology; there is no mention of other characters.	My narrative introduces a character who narrates an experience.	My narrative does not introduce the narrator or any characters.
Situation and Setting	My narrative introduces a setting and situation describing an experience with nanotechnology to orient my readers.	My narrative introduces a situation that describes an experience with nanotechnology.	My narrative introduces a setting, but the situation is unclear.	My narrative does not introduce a setting or a situation.
Experience(s)/ Event(s)	My narrator describes events in an experience with nanotechnology in an order that makes sense.	My narrator describes events in an experience with nanotechnology.	My narrator describes the events of an experience with nanotechnology, but they are not in an order that makes sense.	My narrative does not describe events.
Dialogue and Description	I use dialogue and description to describe an experience with nanotechnology and to show how characters respond.	I use dialogue and description to describe an experience with nanotechnology.	I use dialogue or description to describe an experience.	I do not use dialogue or description adequately to describe an experience.
Details	I include concrete words and sensory details to describe events in my narrative about nanotechnology.	I include concrete words or sensory details to describe events in my narrative about nanotechnology.	I include details to describe events in my narrative about an experience.	I do not include specific details to describe events in my narrative.
Transition Words	I use transition words and phrases to guide readers through the sequence of events.	I use transition words in some places to show the order of events.	I use transition words once or twice to show the order of events.	I do not use transition words to show the order of events.
Conclusion	My narrative has a conclusion that flows naturally from the narrated experience and provides a sense of closure.	My narrative has a conclusion that describes the end of the experience.	My narrative has a conclusion.	My narrative does not have a satisfactory conclusion.

Review

➤ Objective

Students will read a sample narrative essay. Then they will review the characteristics of narrative writing and discuss strengths and weaknesses of the writing with small groups. They will also use their knowledge of narrative writing to write study questions for classmates.

➤ Introduction

You will read a sample narrative essay and refer to the characteristics of narrative writing to identify strengths and weaknesses in the writing. Then you will write study questions for classmates.

➤ Instruction

One way to learn about specific types of writing is to study models. You have learned about the characteristics of narrative writing, or specific things to notice in this type of writing. Read the sample narrative with the categories from the scoring rubrics in mind to identify ways the author included these qualities in his or her writing.

➤ Guided Practice

Distribute "Nanotechnology in the Forest" (page 150) and "Characteristics of Narrative Writing" (page 151). *Read the sample and work with a small group to discuss the strengths and weaknesses of the narrative essay. Refer to the characteristics of narrative writing described on "Self-Evaluation: Narrative Essay" (page 148) to complete Part One. Create a list that details the strengths and weaknesses you observe in the* essay.

➤ Independent Practice

Use your review of the characteristics of narrative writing to create at least five study questions for classmates in Part Two. Your questions may be multiple choice, true/false, fill in the blank, matching, or short answer. Share your questions with a partner for him or her to answer. Then discuss the answers to each other's questions.

➤ Review

Review the characteristics of narrative writing and go over students' evaluations of the sample narrative. As time allows, discuss students' study questions as a class.

➤ Closing

You read a sample narrative and reviewed the characteristics of narrative writing. Then you discussed the strengths and weaknesses of the essay with a small group. You also wrote study questions for classmates to answer and then discussed the answers to your questions.

➤ Answers

"Characteristics of Narrative Writing" (page 151): *Part One*—The opening sentence introduces a character and setting; it could be more specific in introducing the situation and more engaging for readers; The structure of the essay is such that there isn't a full introductory paragraph; body paragraphs would be stronger with more action; body paragraphs have dialogue that makes sense, and the characters interact with one another; the essay includes some descriptive words but very few transition words; the conclusion suggests a solution to the character's situation and provides new insight for the character and readers.

Nanotechnology in the Forest

Samantha spun around in awe, taking in the towering Douglas fir and hemlock trees. "I've never seen such giant trees!"

"I love hiking out here in the wilderness," Ryan said, dragging his feet through the debris on the trail so that all the needles and leaves crackled and crunched.

"I agree, the United States forest land is pretty amazing," their guide, Nicolas, said. "It provides a habitat for animals, clean water for everyone, and industry for small communities, as well." He led them across a sturdy wooden foot bridge over a creek that flowed swiftly with spring run-off. The noise of the water as it tumbled over rocks almost muffled Ryan's next words.

"My dad worked at a lumber mill until he was laid off when it was shut down," said Ryan sadly.

"That must have been difficult for your family," Nicolas sympathized. "It's true that forests have changed quite a bit in the last decade. Have you heard of the new nanomaterial scientists have created from trees and plants?"

"No," said Samantha. "What's nanomaterial?"

Ryan picked up a branch and dragged it behind him for a few paces before standing it upright as a walking stick. "Nano means small, as in atoms and molecules."

"Yes, Ryan, extremely small," said Nicolas. "One nanometer is 1 millionth thickness of a dime! A scientist arranges individual atoms to make nano material, some of which comes from wood pulp."

"Oh, wow!" said Samantha. She bent over to investigate a miniscule fern starting amongst the mulch of the forest floor.

"What do scientists and other people use nanomaterials for?" asked Ryan.

Nicolas patted his forest-ranger vest. "Well, it's very durable and lightweight. Even stronger than bullet-proof vests!"

"Will police officers and detectives wear vests made out of the materials?" Ryan wondered.

"That might be a good purpose for this technology." Nicolas paused. "Nanoparticles can also be used in paint or sprayed on paper to make it more water resistant, or in things like cement to make it lighter."

"They can produce all that from trees?" Samantha patted the trunk of an enormous tree alongside the trail.

Nicolas nodded. "When it's made from trees, it's biodegradable and created from a renewable resource, unlike a lot of synthetic nanomaterials. That makes this nanomaterial very good for the environment, too!"

"Nanotechnology sounds exciting! Maybe in the future I will work in a lumber mill like my dad did, but it would produce nanomaterial!" Ryan grinned.

Teacher Notes
Grade level: below
Lexile estimate: 890L

Name(s): _____

Characteristics of Narrative Writing

➤ Part One

Read "Nanotechnology in the Forest" (page 150). Work with a small group to discuss the strengths and weaknesses of the narrative essay. Refer to the characteristics of narrative writing described on "Self-Evaluation: Narrative Essay" (page 148). As a group, create a list that completes this prompt: This sample essay has the following strengths and weaknesses of narrative writing:

- _____

  _____

- _____

  _____

- _____

  _____

- _____

  _____

- _____

  _____

- _____

  _____

➤ Part Two

Use your review of the characteristics of narrative writing to create at least five study questions for classmates. Your questions may be multiple choice, true/false, fill in the blank, matching, or short answer.

1. _____

2. _____

3. _____

4. _____

5. _____

Share your questions with a partner for him or her to answer on a separate piece of paper. Then discuss the answers to each other's questions.

Final Evaluation

➤ Objective

Students will record and compare the scores they received on their narrative essays from different sources. They will write their observations of what they learned from comparing these scores. Then they will ask and answer reflection questions with classmates.

➤ Introduction

You will compare the scores you received on your writing from different sources. Then you will reflect on the scores and comment on what you learn from your observations. You will also ask and answer reflection questions with a partner.

➤ Instruction

We can use rubrics to observe our writing progress in specific areas over time. During the last two modules, you have learned about and practiced writing narratives. Narrative writing has distinctive characteristics: a narrator, a setting, a description of an experience that includes events that happen in sequential order and sensory details, and an ending that concludes the narrative and reflects on the impact of the experience on the narrator and readers. When we compare scores from pieces we wrote at different times, we see areas in which we have strengthened our writing.

➤ Guided Practice

Distribute "Learning from Evaluations" (page 154) and completed "Teacher Evaluation: Narrative Essay" rubrics (page 153). *Record the scores you received from a classmate on the peer review "Setting Goals for Excellence" (page 146), the scores you gave your writing on "Self-Evaluation: Narrative Essay" (page 148), and the scores you received from me on "Teacher Evaluation: Narrative Essay." How do the scores for each characteristic compare? Which areas of your writing appear to be stronger? In which areas of your writing would you like to continue to improve your skills?*

➤ Independent Practice

Write comments about your scores for each characteristic and what you learned from your observations in the last column of the chart. On the back of the activity page, write two or three reflection questions to ask a classmate. Take turns discussing your responses to each person's reflection questions.

➤ Review

Think aloud to write a comment or observation about what someone might learn from comparing scores from evaluations received on a narrative essay. Then model writing sample reflection questions for students to ask each other.

➤ Closing

You compared the scores you received from different sources on your narrative essay and commented on what you learned from comparing the scores. You then wrote reflection questions for a partner to answer and discussed your answers to a partner's questions.

Teacher Evaluation: Narrative Essay

Student Name: _____   **Score:** _____

	4	3	2	1
Narrator and/ or Characters	The narrative introduces a narrator and/or characters who had an experience with nanotechnology.	The narrative introduces a narrator who had an experience with nanotechnology; there is no mention of other characters.	The narrative introduces a character who narrates an experience.	The narrative does not introduce the narrator or any characters.
Situation and Setting	The narrative introduces a setting and situation describing an experience with nanotechnology to orient readers.	The narrative introduces a situation that describes an experience with nanotechnology.	The narrative introduces a setting, but the situation is unclear.	The narrative does not introduce a setting or a situation.
Experience(s)/ Event(s)	The narrator describes events in an experience with nanotechnology in an order that makes sense.	The narrator describes events in an experience with nanotechnology.	The narrator describes the events of an experience with nanotechnology, but they are not in an order that makes sense.	The narrative does not describe events.
Dialogue and Description	The author uses dialogue and description to describe an experience with nanotechnology and to show how characters respond.	The author uses dialogue and description to describe an experience with nanotechnology.	The author uses dialogue or description to describe an experience.	The author does not use dialogue or description adequately to describe an experience.
Details	The author includes concrete words and sensory details to describe events in the narrative about nanotechnology.	The author includes concrete words or sensory details to describe events in the narrative about nanotechnology.	The author includes details to describe events in the narrative about an experience.	The author does not include specific details to describe events in the narrative.
Transition Words	The author uses transition words and phrases to guide readers through the sequence of events.	The author uses transition words in some places to show the order of events.	The author uses transition words once or twice to show the order of events.	The author does not use transition words to show the order of events.
Conclusion	The narrative has a conclusion that flows naturally from the narrated experience and provides a sense of closure.	The narrative has a conclusion that describes the end of the experience.	The narrative has a conclusion.	The narrative does not have a satisfactory conclusion.

Name(s): _____

Learning from Evaluations

Characteristic	Peer Review Score	Self-Evaluation Score	Teacher Evaluation Score	What I Learned
Narrator and/or Characters				
Situation and Setting				
Experience(s)/ Event(s)				
Dialogue and Description				
Details				
Transition Words				
Conclusion				

Writing Topics

➤ Opinion/Argumentative Writing

Module 1: Interesting Jobs

As a class, explore one or more of the following general career areas:

- Agriculture and food
- Business or management
- Digital and/or print communications
- Education or training
- Government or law
- Health services
- Information technology
- Manufacturing
- Marketing
- Science, technology, engineering, or mathematics (STEM)
- Transportation

Module 2: Current Events or Issues

As a class, focus on current events or issues associated with the following general categories:

- Economics and jobs
- Education
- Environment
- Healthcare
- Human rights in majority and minority groups
- Hunger and poverty
- International events
- Violence or crime in our society

➤ Informative/Explanatory Writing

Module 3: Online Communities

- Social media
- Benefits and risks of online communities
- Purposes of online communities
- Online forums
- Blogs
- Collaborative communities
- Email

Writing Topics *(cont.)*

➤ Informative/Explanatory Writing *(cont.)*

Module 4: Virtual Reality

- Virtual-reality headsets
- Virtual reality in the classroom
- Benefits and risks of virtual reality
- Various uses of virtual-reality headsets

➤ Narrative Writing

Module 5: Volunteer Experiences

- Volunteering at school
- Volunteering in the community
- Volunteering with family
- Volunteering with a group
- Random acts of kindness

Module 6: Nanotechnology

Background information: Nanotechnology is the science of working with very small particles. Atoms and molecules behave differently at the nano scale. A sheet of newspapers is 100,000 nanometers (nm) thick. One nm is 1 billionth (1/1,000,000,000) of a meter.

As a class, explore nanotechnology applications in one or more of the following general areas:

- Computers (e.g., memory, storage capacity, increased speed)
- Medicine
- Electronics
- Robotics
- Energy production (e.g., solar cells)
- Biochemistry
- Mechanical engineering
- Physics

Meeting Standards

Each passage and activity meets one or more of the following Common Core State Standards © Copyright 2010. National Governors Association Center for Best Practices and Council of Chief State School Officers. All rights reserved. For more information about the Common Core State Standards, go to http://www.corestandards.org/ or http://www.teachercreated.com/standards/.

Reading: Literature	Activities
Key Ideas and Details	
RL.6.1: Cite textual evidence to support analysis of what the text says explicitly as well as inferences drawn from the text.	Characteristics of Narrative Writing (M6)
RL.6.2: Determine a theme or central idea of a text and how it is conveyed through particular details; provide a summary of the text distinct from personal opinions or judgments.	Characteristics of Narrative Writing (M6)
RL.6.3: Describe how a particular story's or drama's plot unfolds in a series of episodes as well as how the characters respond or change as the plot moves toward a resolution.	Define Narrative Writing (M5) Characteristics of Narrative Writing (M6)
Craft and Structure	
RL.6.4: Determine the meaning of words and phrases as they are used in a text, including figurative and connotative meanings; analyze the impact of a specific word choice on meaning and tone.	Word Connotations (M5)
RL.6.5: Analyze how a particular sentence, chapter, scene, or stanza fits into the overall structure of a text and contributes to the development of the theme, setting, or plot.	A Satisfactory Conclusion (M5) Define Narrative Writing (M5) Characteristics of Narrative Writing (M6)
RL.6.6: Explain how an author develops the point of view of the narrator or speaker in a text.	Define Narrative Writing (M5) Characteristics of Narrative Writing (M6)

Reading: Informational Text	Activities
Key Ideas and Details	
RI.6.1: Cite textual evidence to support analysis of what the text says explicitly as well as inferences drawn from the text.	Valid Points in an Opinion Paragraph (M1) Review the Characteristics of Opinion Writing (M1) Supporting Evidence (M2) Significant Historic Events (M2) Talk About the Issues (M2) Analyze an Informative Paragraph (M3) Investigate Characteristics of a Paragraph (M3) Critique an Informative Essay (M4)
RI.6.2: Determine a central idea of a text and how it is conveyed through particular details; provide a summary of the text distinct from personal opinions or judgments.	Review the Characteristics of Opinion Writing (M1) Significant Historic Events (M2) Analyze an Informative Paragraph (M3) A Strong Concluding Sentence (M3) Explore a Thesis Statement (M4) An Effective Concluding Paragraph (M4) Critique an Informative Essay (M4)
RI.6.3: Analyze in detail how a key individual, event, or idea is introduced, illustrated, and elaborated in a text (e.g., through examples or anecdotes).	Effective Thesis Statements (M2) Talk About the Issues (M2) Evaluating an Opinion Essay (M2) Analyze an Informative Paragraph (M3) Investigate Characteristics of a Paragraph (M3) Critique an Informative Essay (M4)
Craft and Structure	
RI.6.4: Determine the meaning of words and phrases as they are used in a text, including figurative, connotative, and technical meanings.	Significant Historic Events (M2)
RI.6.5: Analyze how a particular sentence, paragraph, chapter, or section fits into the overall structure of a text and contributes to the development of the ideas.	Observe Transitions (M1) An Effective Concluding Sentence (M1) Evaluating an Opinion Essay (M2) Analyze an Informative Paragraph (M3) Investigate Characteristics of a Paragraph (M3) An Effective Concluding Paragraph (M4)
RI.6.6: Determine an author's point of view or purpose in a text and explain how it is conveyed in the text.	Valid Points in an Opinion Paragraph (M1) Review the Characteristics of Opinion Writing (M1) Significant Historic Events (M2) An Engaging Concluding Paragraph (M2) Talk About the Issues (M2) Evaluating an Opinion Essay (M2) Analyze an Informative Paragraph (M3) Critique an Informative Essay (M4)

Reading: Informational Text *(cont.)*	Activities
Integration of Knowledge and Ideas	
RI.6.7: Integrate information presented in different media or formats (e.g., visually, quantitatively) as well as in words to develop a coherent understanding of a topic or issue.	Supporting Evidence (M2)
RI.6.8: Trace and evaluate the argument and specific claims in a text, distinguishing claims that are supported by reasons and evidence from claims that are not.	Review the Characteristics of Opinion Writing (M1) Talk About the Issues (M2) Evaluating an Opinion Essay (M2)
Range of Reading and Level of Text Complexity	
RI.6.10: By the end of the year, read and comprehend literary nonfiction in the grades 6–8 text complexity band proficiently, with scaffolding as needed at the high end of the range.	Valid Points in an Opinion Paragraph (M1)

Writing	Activities
Text Types and Purposes	
W.6.1: Write arguments to support claims with clear reasons and relevant evidence.	My Opinions (M1) An Interesting Topic Sentence (M1) Support Your Opinion (M1) Gather the Evidence (M1) Observe Transitions (M1) An Effective Concluding Sentence (M1) Write a Concluding Sentence (M1) First Draft and Peer Review (M1) Second Draft and Self-Evaluation (M1) Final Draft (M1) Effective Thesis Statements (M2) Perspectives on My Topic (M2) A Captivating Introductory Paragraph (M2) Supporting Evidence (M2) Develop an Opposing Argument (M2) An Engaging Concluding Paragraph (M2) First Draft and Peer Review (M2) Second Draft and Self-Evaluation (M2)
W.6.2: Write informative/explanatory texts to examine a topic and convey ideas, concepts, and information through the selection, organization, and analysis of relevant content.	Introduce Your Topic (M3) Facts & Details (M3) Specific Details (M3) Connect with Your Audience (M3) Connected Ideas (M3) A Strong Concluding Sentence (M3) First Draft and Peer Review (M3) Second Draft and Self-Evaluation (M3) Final Draft (M3) Explore a Thesis Statement (M4) Map Your Concept (M4) Research Your Topic (M4) Planning My Essay (M4) Focus on Details (M4) An Effective Concluding Paragraph (M4) Write a Concluding Paragraph (M4) First Draft and Peer Review (M4) Second Draft and Self-Evaluation (M4)
W.6.3: Write narratives to develop real or imagined experiences or events using effective technique, relevant descriptive details, and well-structured event sequences.	Introduce a Character (M5) Orient Readers (M5) Actions Within the Experience (M5) Helping Hands (M5) Getting Around My Narrative (M5) A Satisfactory Conclusion (M5) Making a Difference (M5) First Draft and Peer Review (M5) My Writing Group (M5) Second Draft and Self-Evaluation (M5) Final Draft (M5) Planning My Narrative (M6) Engage Readers (M6) Describing an Experience (M6) Actions and Reactions (M6) My Response Is . . . (M6) Connect to Readers (M6)

Meeting Standards (cont.)

Writing (cont.)	Activities
Text Types and Purposes (cont.)	
W.6.3: Write narratives to develop real or imagined experiences or events using effective technique, relevant descriptive details, and well-structured event sequences. (cont.)	A Meaningful Conclusion (M6) First Draft and Peer Review (M6) Second Draft and Self-Evaluation (M6)
Production and Distribution of Writing	
W.6.4: Produce clear and coherent writing in which the development, organization, and style are appropriate to task, purpose, and audience.	Support Your Opinion (M1) Final Draft (M1) A Captivating Introductory Paragraph (M2) Develop an Opposing Argument (M2) An Engaging Concluding Paragraph (M2) Second Draft and Self-Evaluation (M2) Connect with Your Audience (M3) A Strong Concluding Sentence (M3) First Draft and Peer Review (M3) Final Draft (M3) Writers and Readers (M3) An Effective Concluding Paragraph (M4) Write a Concluding Paragraph (M4) Second Draft and Self-Evaluation (M4) Critique an Informative Essay (M4) Second Draft and Self-Evaluation (M5) Final Draft (M5) Engage Readers (M6) A Meaningful Conclusion (M6) First Draft and Peer Review (M6) Second Draft and Self-Evaluation (M6) Characteristics of Narrative Writing (M6)
W.6.5: With some guidance and support from peers and adults, develop and strengthen writing as needed by planning, revising, editing, rewriting, or trying a new approach.	Observe Transitions (M1) Write a Concluding Sentence (M1) Check My Writing (M1) Steps to Great Writing (M1) Final Draft (M1) Different Perspectives (M1) A Captivating Introductory Paragraph (M2) Develop an Opposing Argument (M2) An Engaging Concluding Paragraph (M2) A Focused Review (M2) Second Draft and Self-Evaluation (M2) Evaluating an Opinion Essay (M2) An Exchange of Ideas (M3) Connect with Your Audience (M3) Connected Ideas (M3) A Strong Concluding Sentence (M3) Moving Toward Excellence (M3) Evaluating My Writing (M3) Writers and Readers (M3) Graphing My Progress (M3) Explore a Thesis Statement (M4) Planning My Essay (M4) Focus on Details (M4) Write a Concluding Paragraph (M4) Strengthen Your Writing (M4) Second Draft and Self-Evaluation (M4) Introduce a Character (M5) Orient Readers (M5) Helping Hands (M5) Word Connotations (M5) Getting Around My Narrative (M5) Making a Difference (M5) My Writing Group (M5) Second Draft and Self-Evaluation (M5) Grab Your Audience (M5) Steps Toward Mastery (M5) Planning My Narrative (M6) Engage Readers (M6) Describing an Experience (M6) Actions and Reactions (M6)

Meeting Standards (cont.)

Writing (cont.)	Activities
Production and Distribution of Writing (cont.)	
W.6.5: With some guidance and support from peers and adults, develop and strengthen writing as needed by planning, revising, editing, rewriting, or trying a new approach. *(cont.)*	My Response Is . . . (M6) Connect to Readers (M6) A Meaningful Conclusion (M6) Setting Goals for Excellence (M6) Second Draft and Self-Evaluation (M6) Learning from Evaluations (M6)
W.6.6: Use technology, including the Internet, to produce and publish writing as well as to interact and collaborate with others; demonstrate sufficient command of keyboarding skills to type a minimum of three pages in a single sitting.	Final Draft (M1) Second Draft and Self-Evaluation (M2) Final Draft (M3) An Effective Concluding Paragraph (M4) Second Draft and Self-Evaluation (M4) My Writing Group (M5) Final Draft (M5) Second Draft and Self-Evaluation (M6)
Research to Build and Present Knowledge	
W.6.7: Conduct short research projects to answer a question, drawing on several sources and refocusing the inquiry when appropriate.	Gather the Evidence (M1) Supporting Evidence (M2) Develop an Opposing Argument (M2) Facts & Details (M3) Specific Details (M3) Research Your Topic (M4)
W.6.8: Gather relevant information from multiple print and digital sources; assess the credibility of each source; and quote or paraphrase the data and conclusions of others while avoiding plagiarism and providing basic bibliographic information for sources.	Gather the Evidence (M1) Supporting Evidence (M2) Facts & Details (M3) Research Your Topic (M4)
W.6.9: Draw evidence from literary or informational texts to support analysis, reflection, and research.	Support Your Opinion (M1) Gather the Evidence (M1) Supporting Evidence (M2) Facts & Details (M3) Specific Details (M3) Research Your Topic (M4)
Range of Writing	
W.6.10: Write routinely over extended time frames (time for research, reflection, and revision) and shorter time frames (a single sitting or a day or two) for a range of discipline-specific tasks, purposes, and audiences.	*all*

Language	Activities
Conventions of Standard English	
L.6.1: Demonstrate command of the conventions of standard English grammar and usage when writing or speaking.	*all*
L.6.2: Demonstrate command of the conventions of standard English capitalization, punctuation, and spelling when writing.	*all*
Knowledge of Language	
L.6.3: Use knowledge of language and its conventions when writing, speaking, reading, or listening.	*all*
Vocabulary Acquisition and Use	
L.6.4: Determine or clarify the meaning of unknown and multiple-meaning words and phrases based on grade 6 reading and content, choosing flexibly from a range of strategies.	Observe Transitions (M1) Significant Historic Events (M2) Specific Details (M3) Introduce a Character (M5) Helping Hands (M5) Word Connotations (M5) Describing an Experience (M6)
L.6.5: Demonstrate understanding of figurative language, word relationships, and nuances in word meanings.	Specific Details (M3) Connect with Your Audience (M3) Focus on Details (M4) Introduce a Character (M5) Orient Readers (M5) Helping Hands (M5) Word Connotations (M5) Describing an Experience (M6)
L.6.6: Acquire and use accurately grade-appropriate general academic and domain-specific words and phrases; gather vocabulary knowledge when considering a word or phrase important to comprehension or expression.	*all*